Third Edition

Overcoming

Prescription Drug Addiction

A Guide to Coping and Understanding

Rod Colvin, M.S.

Addicus Books, Inc.
Omaha, Nebraska

An Addicus Nonfiction Book

ISBN: 978-1-886039-88-9
Cover design by Peri Poloni
Typography by Linda Dageforde

The second edition of this book was published as *Prescription Drug Addiction—The Hidden Epidemic*, 2002. ISBN: 1-886039-52-6

This book is not intended as a substitute for a physician. Nor is it the author's intent to provide medical advice.

Library of Congress Cataloging-in-Publication Data

Colvin, Rod
Overcoming prescription drug addiction : a guide to coping and understanding / Rod Colvin. — [3rd ed.]
p. cm.
"An Addicus Nonfiction Book."
Previously published as: Prescription drug addiction : the hidden epidemic, c2002.
Includes index.
ISBN 978-1-886039-88-9 (alk. paper)
1. Medication abuse. 2. Drug abuse. I. Colvin, Rod, Prescription drug addiction. II. Title.
RM146.5.C65 2008
362.29'9—dc22 2008026242

Addicus Books, Inc.
P.O. Box 45327
Omaha, Nebraska 68145
www.AddicusBooks.com

Printed in the United States of America
10 9 8 7 6 5 4 3 2 1

To the memory
of my brother Randy

Contents

Acknowledgments

I would like to express my appreciation to the many people who shared their time and expertise, helping to make this book possible. A note of special thanks goes to all those who shared their personal stories of recovery. Your voices will resonate among those who still suffer.

The many others I wish to thank include: Edward Covington, M.D., Cleveland Clinic; Bill White, Chestnut Health Systems; Tim Lepak, National Association for Advocates of Buprenorphine Treatment; Don Vogt, Oklahoma Prescription Drug Monitoring Program; David Hopkins, Kentucky Prescription Drug Monitoring Program; Sgt. Stan Salyards, Louisville Police Department; Sgt. Harvey Smith, Virginia State Police; Dale Smith, Westshore, Ohio, Enforcement Bureau; Capt. Richard Conklin, Stamford Police Department; Shelly Burgess, Substance Abuse and Mental Health Services; Jeff Baldwin, Pharm. D., University of Nebraska; Clifford Bernstein, M.D., Waismann Institute; Milton Birnbaum, M.D.; LeClair Bissell, M.D.; Sheila Blume, M.D.; Ed Hughes, Executive Director, The Counseling Center, Inc.

Ray Bullman, National Council on Patient Information and Education; John Burke, President, National Association of Drug Diversion Investigators; Carol Colleran, Hanley Center; Bruce Cotter, Interventionist; Patrick Dalton, Addiction Institute; Robert L. DuPont, M.D.; Betty Ferrell, Ph.D.; David

Gastfriend, M.D.; Ronald Gershman, M.D.; Terence Gorski, Relapse Prevention Expert; Sherry Green, Executive Director, National Alliance for Model State Drug Laws; Howard Heit, M.D.; Jeff Jay, President, Terry McGovern Foundation.

David Joranson, Pain Research Group, University of Wisconsin; David Mee-Lee, M.D.; John Mudri, Retired, DEA Diversion Investigator; Sidney Schnoll, M.D.; David Smith, M.D.; Myron Weiner, M.D.; Bonnie Wilford, Medical Education Consultant; Steffie Woolhandler, M.D.; Bob Pack, Troy and Alana Pack Foundation; James Giglio, Director, New York Bureau of Narcotic Enforcement; Mark Parrino, American Association for the Treatment of Opioid Dependence, Paul Bowman, National Alliance of Methadone Advocates.

Finally, I would like to thank Jack Kusler, Susan Adams, and Betty Wright, whose ongoing support helped make this book possible.

Introduction

My Story

I wrapped my birthday gift, and left it on the kitchen table. As I headed to work, I casually pondered which restaurant to take my brother Randy to. The upcoming evening was to be one of celebration. Not only had Randy just completed his college degree in business, but today he was turning thirty-five. A celebration birthday dinner was definitely in order. But around noon, I got a telephone call at my office. It was a nurse from nearby Methodist Hospital.

"Are you the brother of Randy?" she asked after identifying herself.

"Yes," I said, as my head began to spin. I wondered what had happened.

"Your brother has been brought in by a rescue squad... he's in critical condition."

The nurse gave me no other details—she just asked me to come at once.

Terrified, I jumped in the car and sped toward the hospital. "God, please don't take my brother," I prayed aloud as I raced toward the hospital. Minutes later, I was in the emergency room. Frantically, I was scanning the bays of beds, looking for Randy, but I didn't see him anywhere.

Just then, a nurse approached me. "Are you Randy's brother?" she asked.

"Yes," I said.

"Let's step out into the hall," she said.

My heart sank. At that moment, I knew the worst had happened. "Is he dead?" I asked, not wanting to hear her response.

The nurse dropped her gaze and nodded. Randy was gone.

The death of my brother—and only sibling—was one of the most profound losses of my life, but I must tell you, his early passing was not a total shock. For years, Randy had battled a prescription drug dependency that started at age twenty when a psychiatrist first prescribed tranquilizers to help him cope with anxiety. The drugs made him feel good, so he started using them more and more. Over the years, he became very clever in obtaining Valium, Xanax, Percodan, Percocet, and other painkillers by a common scam known as "doctor shopping." He would visit multiple doctors and feign back pain and ask for relief. He had also learned that on weekends, he could go to hospital emergency rooms, where it was easier to go unnoticed in the whirl of activity. There, he would ask for painkillers for a bad toothache, explaining that his dentist was not available until Monday.

My parents and I had long feared the toll this behavior was taking on him emotionally and physically. It was so painful for us to watch his bouts with addiction and his refusal to get help. He ruined many holidays, including Christmas dinners, showing up "drunk" on pills. Repeatedly, we had pleaded with Randy to get help—even offered to pay for treatment—but he always denied that he had a problem. Any suggestion that he had a drug problem angered him.

Still, at times over the years, he appeared to be leaving the drugs behind—he would be clearheaded and showed no signs of abusing drugs. He even enrolled in college. Each time we observed such positive changes, we thought he had beaten the problem. In fact, just before he died, he had been drug free for nearly a year. It was a sure sign, we thought, that addiction was part of his past. However, as I later pieced together the last hours of his life, I learned that he had relapsed—prescription drugs, mixed with alcohol, a dangerous combination, had contributed to Randy's death. The autopsy revealed that he didn't die of an overdose, but rather he had gone into cardiac arrest. He died in his sleep while taking a nap at a friend's house. The years of drug abuse had simply taken a toll on his heart.

My brother's long battle—our family's agonizing battle—with prescription drug dependency was over. Sadly, we had lost. Randy died on October 19, 1988—his thirty-fifth birthday.

Cherishing the Memories

In the years since my brother died, I've healed from the acute pain of the loss, but I still feel the loss deeply. When he was not drug affected, he was a kind, caring young man. I miss reminiscing with him. We used to call each other, laughing about funny stories from childhood. I miss those calls. And I often wonder if he were alive today, what he might be doing professionally—he was such a bright guy. And I think about what we might chat about over coffee—politics, the vast world of technology and the Internet, our fields of work?

Left now with only memories, I'm especially grateful for an experience I had with him shortly before his death. I'd had minor surgery, and Randy drove me home from the clinic. He fixed me a bite to eat and stayed close by while I napped. He seemed to enjoy being the caretaker, the role I was so used to playing with him. "It's so nice to have a brother," I said. He just smiled and patted me on the shoulder. It's a memory I'll treasure always.

Randy was only one of millions of people who started taking prescription drugs for legitimate medical reasons and progressed to addiction. Today, prescription drug abuse is one of the nation's most serious drug problems, and the results can be deadly. This growing problem claims victims from all walks of life.

—Rod Colvin

Part I

Coping with Addiction

Although the world is full of suffering,
it is full also of overcoming it.

—Helen Keller
1880–1968

1

Understanding Addiction

Somewhere, at this very moment, a man's wife agonizes as she receives a call from the police—her husband has been arrested for forging prescriptions for tranquilizers. In another community, a mother weeps as her adult daughter, intoxicated on painkillers, disrupts yet another family gathering. In a small Midwest town, a family is grieving the death of their teenage son who died at a party from an overdose of prescription anxiety medication and alcohol. The case scenarios go on and on. Legions of Americans are abusing and becoming addicted to prescription drugs.

In fact, chances are you know someone who is abusing prescription drugs. Maybe it's your spouse, a relative, a friend, or a casual acquaintance. Maybe it's you.

Defining Addiction

Addiction is a pattern of compulsive drug use characterized by a continued craving for drugs and the need to use these drugs for psychological effects or mood alterations. Many abusers find that they need to use drugs to feel "normal." The user exhibits drug-seeking behavior and is often preoccupied with using and obtaining the drugs of choice. These substances may be obtained through legal or illegal channels.

The American Society of Addiction Medicine considers addiction "a disease process characterized by the continued use of a specific psychoactive substance despite physical, psychological, or social harm." Addiction is a chronic disease that is progressive—it worsens over time. It can be diagnosed and treated, but without treatment, it is ultimately fatal.

How Addiction Affects the Brain

It was once thought that addiction was a result of being weak-willed—addicts could stop using drugs if they *wanted* to. But research has shown that this is not the case. In fact, after prolonged use of an addictive substance, the "circuits" in the brain virtually become "rewired."

When a medication enters the brain, it is absorbed through receptor sites. Addictive drugs are believed to act on the brain by reinforcing the action of the body's natural chemical, known as dopamine, that is involved in producing the sensation of pleasure. When the body is getting such chemicals from an outside source, the brain stops making some of its own and becomes dependent on the outside source. As the brain adapts to the drug's presence, the individual using the drug builds tolerance and must continually increase the dosage in order to achieve the initial pleasure sensations. However, most addicts in recovery report that they rarely achieved that initial sense of euphoria or feeling of well-being again.

Further, if the drug is stopped abruptly, it usually triggers a withdrawal syndrome. Symptoms of withdrawal may vary depending on the length of the addiction and the drug being used, but common symptoms from painkillers may include anxiety, irritability, chills alternating with hot flashes, salivation, nausea, abdominal cramps, or even death. Some individuals describe withdrawal as the worst possible flu you can imagine. As one goes into withdrawal, the body "begs" for more of the addictive drug in order to escape the misery. Understandably, giving up the drug is difficult.

This inability to stop using the drug is a characteristic of addiction. Although an addicted individual may intellectually understand the destructive consequences of addiction, he or she may not be able to stop the compulsive use of a drug; the changes in brain structure can affect emotions and motivation, both of which affect behavior.

Another common characteristic of addiction, *denial,* makes it even more difficult for the addicted individual to give up a drug. Denial refers to the addict's belief that he or she really does not have a drug problem. This self-protective mechanism is governed by the subconscious areas of the brain where the main addiction pathways exist. Denial keeps the addict from acknowledging both the drug problem and the underlying emotional issues that may be influencing the use of drugs. Usually, the longer the drug abuse has gone on, the stronger the denial.

Drug Misuse

There are levels of drug abuse. *Drug misuse* refers to drugs unintentionally being used improperly by people hoping to get a therapeutic benefit from the drugs. Misuse includes many scenarios, ranging from the patient who stops taking a medication on his or her own, to the patient who may be exchanging drugs with family members or friends.

Medication misuse causes thousands of deaths and hospitalizations each year, and the cost to the economy is in the billions of dollars.

Another potentially fatal misuse of drugs involves painkillers or sedatives taken in combination with alcohol. Even though a drinker may have developed a tolerance to the sedative effects of alcohol, he or she will not have developed a tolerance for the alcohol's depressing effects on the respiratory system. The combination of alcohol and tranquilizers or sedatives can create cardiorespiratory depression and lead to death.

Drug Abuse

Drug abuse refers to "the use, usually by self-administration, of any drug in a manner that deviates from the approved medical use or social patterns within a given culture. The term conveys the notion of social disapproval, and it is not necessarily descriptive of any particular pattern of drug use or its potential adverse consequences," according to *The Pharmacological Basis of Therapeutics* by Jerome Jaffe. Drug abuse may include using a medication "recreationally," using it for reasons other than those intended, or using the drug more frequently than indicated by the prescriber. Abuse may or may not involve addiction.

It is estimated that as much as 28 percent of all prescribed controlled substances are abused. That estimate translates to tens of millions of drug doses being diverted annually for the purpose of abuse. *Diversion* refers to the redirecting of drugs from legitimate use into illicit channels. The drugs may be obtained through any number of sources—by bogus prescriptions, from a friend, or purchased on the streets.

How Many Americans Are Abusing Prescription Drugs?

It's difficult to say with precision just how many Americans are abusing prescription drugs, although estimates are available. According to 2007 statistics, nearly 17 million Americans aged twelve or older reported having used prescription drugs—painkillers, sedatives, tranquilizers, or stimulants—for nonmedical purposes during the year. In fact, the number of people abusing prescription drugs is greater than the combined number of people using cocaine, hallucinogens, inhalants, and heroin. Overall, 56 percent more Americans abuse prescription drugs than these illegal drugs.

Teen Abuse on the Rise

Prescription drug abuse among teenagers has tripled since 1992. Today, nearly 19 percent of all teens report having taken a painkiller for nonmedical purposes. Prescription drug abuse among college students is estimated at 20 percent.

The National Center on Addiction and Substance Abuse at Columbia University reports that more than half the nation's twelve-to-seventeen-year-olds are at risk of substance abuse because of high stress, frequent boredom, too much spending money, or a combination thereof. Unfortunately, many teens believe that prescription drugs, such as painkillers, are safer than illegal street drugs, and many are not aware of the addiction risks associated with narcotics. Many teens report getting drugs from their family medicine chest or from friends.

Statistics on Teen Drug Abuse

- One in five teens (19 percent) have used prescription drugs to get high.
- One in four teens report having a friend who uses pills to get high.
- One in three teens report being offered pills for recreational use.
- Every day, 2,700 teens try a prescription drug for the first time to get high.

Source: Partnership for a Drug-Free America

Emergency Room Visits on the Rise

The number of prescription drug abusers seeking treatment in emergency rooms is also on the rise. In 2005, drug and alcohol abuse sent nearly 1.5 million people to hospital emergency rooms. To make the magnitude of this statistic more real, imagine every man, woman, and child in the city of Philadelphia going to a hospital emergency room as the result of substance abuse.

Overdoses on the Rise

Fatal poisonings from drug overdoses are rising dramatically in the United States. Officials say most of these deaths are from prescription drugs rather than illegal drugs such as heroin. According to the Centers for Disease Control (CDC), more than 33,000 Americans died of drug overdoses in 2005, the most recent year for which statistics are available. This number makes drug overdose the second leading cause of accidental death. (Traffic accidents are the leading cause of accidental deaths.)

In 1990, the CDC reported 10,000 drug overdose deaths; in 1999, the number was 20,000. The 2005 death toll represents a 60 percent increase in drug-related deaths between 2000 and 2005. The government estimates that such abuse costs about a half trillion dollars a year, or about $1,650 per American.

Addiction Rate in the United States

It's generally believed that between 10 and 16 percent of Americans are chemically dependent at some point in life. These percentages refer to all addictive substances, including alcohol, prescription medications, and illegal substances, but do not include tobacco. Many individuals in recovery report that they often used both alcohol and prescription drugs, depending on their availability. A 1998 report by the University of Chicago states that multidrug consumption is the normal pattern among a broad range of substance abusers.

Symptoms of Addiction

Prescription drug abuse is often difficult for friends and family to recognize. Contrary to popular belief, one need not abuse drugs daily to have a problem with addiction; the pattern of abuse may be occasional or habitual. The abuse is usually an intensely private affair between the abuser and a bottle of pills. And the pill taker is not subject to the social stigma associated with the shadowy world of street-drug dealing. Still, the following are symptoms of addiction:

- Showing relief from anxiety
- Changes in mood—from a sense of well-being to belligerence
- False feelings of self-confidence
- Increased sensitivity to sights and sounds, including hallucinations
- Slurred speech and poor motor control
- Decline in hygiene and appearance
- Altered activity levels—such as sleeping for twelve to fourteen hours or frenzied activity lasting for hours
- Lack of interest in activities previously enjoyed
- Unpleasant or painful symptoms when the substance is withdrawn
- Preoccupation with running out of pills

Who's at Risk for Addiction?

Who is at risk for addiction? Medical science has also determined that those with a family history of addictions have

Distinguishing Medical Use of Drugs from Nonmedical Substance Use

	Medical Use	Nonmedical Use
Intent	To treat diagnosed illness	To alter mood
Effect	Makes life of user better	Makes life of user worse
Pattern	Steady and sensible	Chaotic and high dose
Legality	Legal	Illegal (except alcohol or tobacco use by adults)
Control	Shared with physician	Self-controlled

From "Benzodiazepines, Addiction and Public Policy," by Robert L. DuPont, M.D., *New Jersey Medicine*, 90 (1993): 824-826. Reprinted by permission.

about a threefold greater risk of developing addictions. But, in addition to family history, there are other risk factors.

The risk for addiction is greatest among women, seniors, and, as mentioned earlier, teenagers. Women are two to three times more likely than men to be prescribed drugs such as sedatives; they are also about two times more likely to become addicted. This stems in large part from the fact that women are more likely to seek medical attention for emotional problems. Seniors take more drugs than the rest of the population and have a reduced capability of breaking them down and eliminating them; this increases their odds of becoming addicted. And the surge in teenage abuse of prescription drugs has led to dependency among many. Other groups at increased risk for addiction are medical professionals, alcoholics, and smokers.

Other factors that put one at risk for addiction include:

- Medical condition that requires pain medication
- Extreme stress from family tragedy or death
- Divorce
- Excessive alcohol consumption
- Fatigue or overwork
- Poverty
- Depression
- Dependency
- Poor self-image
- Obesity

Is everyone who takes addictive drugs at risk for addiction? The answer is no. "Twenty years ago, it was widely believed that virtually anyone who took psychoactive drugs was a likely candidate for dependency, but that thinking has changed," states Bonnie Wilford, Executive Director of the Alliance for Prescription Drug Abuse Prevention. "Our change of thought has come about as a result of our increased knowledge about addiction. For example, perhaps seven out of ten people could take tranquilizers and not progress to addiction. But those who do become addicted likely have a preexisting addictive disorder, such as predisposition to alcoholism. The difficulty is, we don't always know which patients this will be."

The "Unwitting" Addict

Many individuals who become dependent on prescription drugs are "unwitting" addicts. These are individuals who have no prior history of drug abuse or addiction. They started using a prescribed drug for a legitimate problem, physical or emotional. For example, it may have been a painkiller for a back injury or a sedative for anxiety. Then, at some point, these individuals started increasing the dosages on their own because the drug made them feel better—giving them relief from physical or emotional distress. The nature of the drug required that they continue escalating the dosages to get the desired effect. Gradually, the abuse became full-blown addiction.

Which Drugs Are Being Abused?

According to the Drug Abuse Warning Network, prescription drugs are among the most abused substances in the United States; these drugs are abused more than heroin and cocaine combined. Only marijuana use is more common than prescription drug abuse.

At the top of the list of prescription drugs being abused are benzodiazepines and painkillers. The Drug Abuse Warning Network keeps a ranking of such drugs, based on information gathered during hospital emergency room visits across the nation. The patient must indicate that a drug was being used for purposes of recreation or dependence in order for the episode to be considered drug abuse.

Commonly Abused Prescription Drugs

Opioids

Opioids, more commonly known as painkillers, belong to a class of drugs also known as *opiates* and are typically prescribed to relieve acute or chronic pain, such as that from cancer or surgery. These drugs are also referred to as *narcotic analgesics* or pain relievers. For acute pain, opioids are normally used only for short periods—fewer than thirty days. Opioids may be taken orally or by injection.

Although they are medically indicated for the control of pain, opioids are drugs with high abuse potential. In addition to blocking pain messages being sent to the brain, opioids produce feelings of euphoria or pleasure. It is this sensation that makes the drug highly sought after by those wishing to free themselves from painful emotions. Chronic use of opioids results in both tolerance and dependence.

Common opioid products include:

- Darvocet-N
- Darvon
- Demerol
- Dilaudid
- Lorcet
- Lortab
- Methadone
- Morphine
- OxyContin
- Percocet
- Percodan
- Roxicet
- Roxiprin
- Tussionex
- Tylenol with Codeine
- Vicodin

According to the National Institute on Drug Abuse, the number of opioid prescriptions in the United States escalated from nearly 40 million in 1991 to 180 million in 2007. That's an increase of 350 percent at a time when the population increased by 19 percent.

Opioid Withdrawal

Stopping the use of opioids suddenly will bring on symptoms of withdrawal. Initial withdrawal symptoms usually begin within hours of the last dose and may include: cravings,

Most Abused Prescription Drugs in the United States

1. Alprazolam *(Xanax)*
2. Hydrocodone *(Lorcet, Lortab, Vicodin)*
3. Unspecified benzodiazepines
4. Oxycodone *(OxyContin, Percocet, Percodan, Tylox)*
5. Methadone
6. Clonazepam *(Klonopin)*
7. Propoxyphene *(Darvocet-N, Darvon)*
8. Amphetamine *(Dexedrine)*
9. Lorazepam *(Ativan)*
10. Carisoprodol *(Soma)*
11. Diazepam *(Valium)*
12. Methamphetamine *(Desoxyn, speed)*
13. Trazodone *(Desyrel)*

Source: From Drug Abuse Warning Network Emergency Room Data. Based on drugs mentioned during emergency room visits in 2005.

running nose, excessive sweating, insomnia, and violent yawning. Those who have been addicted to opioids for a long time may progress to severe withdrawal symptoms, including: chills, fever, muscle spasms, and abdominal pain. Opioid withdrawal is rarely fatal.

Cessation of opioids is best accomplished under medical supervision, where withdrawal can be managed. A medically assisted withdrawal is safer and also increases the chance that an individual will "come off" a drug.

Stimulants

Stimulants are drugs that stimulate the central nervous system, increasing mental alertness, decreasing fatigue, and producing a sense of well-being. These drugs are often prescribed for attention deficit (hyperactivity or ADHD) disorder and narcolepsy, a condition characterized by excessive daytime sleepiness, even after adequate nighttime sleep. Common stimulation drugs include:

- Adderall
- Concerta
- Cylert
- Dexedrine
- Ritalin

Interestingly, while the drugs listed above stimulate the central nervous system in adults, they have a calming effect on children. Consequently, these stimulants are often prescribed for children diagnosed with ADHD. The drugs produce a calming effect in these children by stimulating nerves that slow down other overactive nerves.

In adults, other stimulants such as Adipex-P, Bontril, Didrex, Ionamin, Meridia, Prelu-2, Pro-Fast, and Tenuate may be used to suppress appetite.

Stimulants such as Dexedrine and Ritalin increase the amount of the natural brain chemicals *norepinephrine* and *dopamine*. The increased levels of these chemicals create both an increased heart rate and increased blood pressure and a sense of pleasure, resulting in an overall sense of heightened energy and sense of well-being. Once accustomed to an outside source of these chemicals, the body craves more of them.

Anyone taking high doses of stimulants runs the risk of irregular heartbeat and high blood pressure, which can result in heart failure. High doses may also result in feelings of hostility and paranoia.

Stimulant Withdrawal

Symptoms of withdrawal from stimulants include: depression, fatigue, loss of interest or pleasure in daily activities, insomnia, loss of appetite, suicidal thoughts and behavior, and paranoid delusions.

Sedatives

Sedatives are drugs that depress the central nervous system and are frequently used to treat anxiety, panic disorder, or insomnia; some are also used for seizure disorders. As these drugs interact with chemicals in the brain, they cause a reduction in brain activity and bring about the sedative effect.

Benzodiazepines, often referred to as "benzos," are among the most commonly prescribed sedatives. Those often prescribed for daytime use are:

- Ativan
- Serax
- Valium
- Librium
- Tranxene
- Xanax

Benzodiazepines frequently used for nighttime insomnia are:

- Doral
- ProSom
- Halcion
- Restoril

Benzodiazepines used for seizure disorders are:

- Ativan
- Tranxene
- Klonopin
- Valium

Benzodiazepine Abuse

Benzodiazepines are among the most abused prescription drugs in the nation. They were first introduced into American medicine in 1960 to control anxiety. Today, it's estimated that between 10 and 12 percent of the population use benzodiazepines within the course of a year. According to the Drug Abuse Warning Network, most deaths from benzodiazepines are caused by combined use with alcohol.

Short-Term vs. Long-Term Use

Debate continues in the medical community over the safe, long-term use of benzodiazepines, since the buildup of tolerance is often rapid, and severe withdrawal can occur if these drugs are stopped abruptly. Short-term use is considered a few weeks or less; long-term use refers to several months or more. The debate prompted the American Psychiatric Association to issue a statement claiming, "Physiological dependence on benzodiazepines...can develop with therapeutic doses. Duration of treatment determines the onset of dependence...clinically significant dependence usually does not appear before four months of such daily dosing. Dependence may develop sooner when higher, anti-panic doses are taken daily."

Questions Doctors Should Consider before Prescribing Long-Term Use of Benzodiazepines

1. **Diagnosis and response to treatment.** Does the patient have a clear-cut diagnosis, and does the patient respond favorably to the use of the benzodiazepine?
2. **Use of psychotropic substances.** Is the patient's use of alcohol and other substances legal and sensible? Does the patient avoid all use of illegal drugs? Is the benzodiazepine dose reasonable? Is the use of other prescribed drugs medically reasonable?
3. **Toxic behavior.** Is the patient free of slurred speech, accidents, or other problems that may be associated with excessive or inappropriate use of any prescribed or nonprescribed psychoactive substance?
4. **Family monitor.** Does a family member confirm that the patient's use of the benzodiazepine is both sensible and helpful and that the patient does not abuse alcohol or use illegal substances?

A "no" answer to any of these questions suggests the need to discontinue benzodiazepines. A "yes" to all four questions supports continuation of benzodiazepine prescriptions if that is the shared conclusion of the patient and the physician. The standard to be met: Is this treatment clearly in the patient's best interest?

From "Benzodiazepines, Addiction and Public Policy," by Robert L. DuPont, M.D., *New Jersey Medicine* 90 (1993): 824-826. Reprinted by permission.

Benzodiazepine Withdrawal

Symptoms of withdrawal from benzodiazepines and other sedatives include: insomnia, anxiety, depression, euphoria, incoherent thoughts, hostility, grandiosity, disorientation, tactical/auditory/visual hallucinations, and suicidal thoughts. Symptoms can progress to include: abdominal cramps, muscle cramps, nausea or vomiting, trembling, sweats, and seizures.

Anyone who has used benzodiazepines over an extended period of time—several weeks or more—should never stop taking the drug abruptly. After long-term use, medically unsupervised withdrawal can be severe, leading to delirium, fever, seizures, coma, and even death. Individuals wishing to stop the drug should ask their physicians about being medically supervised so that withdrawal can be managed as use of the drug is tapered.

Another symptom of withdrawal is "symptom rebound," an intensified return of the original symptoms (such as insomnia or anxiety) for which the drug was first prescribed. This rebound is often misinterpreted by patients as a recurrence of anxiety.

History of Addiction and Benzodiazepines

Some of the controversy surrounding the use of benzodiazepines has resulted from the dependency problems occurring among patients who have had previous problems with addiction. "Patients who have a history of chemical dependence, including the use of alcohol or drugs, are poor candidates for use of benzodiazepines in the treatment of anxiety," states Robert L. DuPont, M.D., former director of the National Institute on Drug Abuse. "Anyone who has used illicit drugs repeatedly over a period of months or years, and anyone who drinks more than a few drinks of alcohol a week, should use benzodiazepines with extreme caution, if at all."

Distinction between Addiction and Physiological Dependence

Addiction

- Loss of control of drug use
- Continued use despite problems caused by use
- Denial
- Relapse
- A complex, biobehavioral, lifelong, malignant problem
- Limited to chemically dependent people
- Not a complication of medical treatment unless a prior history of chemical dependence exists
- Best treated by specific chemical dependence treatment

Physiological Dependence

- A cellular adaptation to the presence of a substance
- Withdrawal symptoms on abrupt discontinuation
- Not associated with relapse
- A benign, temporary problem
- Common to many substances used in medicine including steroids, antidepressants, and antiepilepsy and antihypertensive medicines
- Best treated by gradual dose reduction

Physiological Dependence and Addiction: The Difference

Not all drug dependence is addiction. *Physiological dependence,* which is often confused with addiction, is a result of the body's adaptation to a drug used over a period of time to treat a medical disorder. For example, a patient taking pain medication for several weeks would likely develop some degree of tolerance to the drug; he or she would become physically dependent, and would have withdrawal symptoms if the drug were stopped abruptly. This type of dependence, however, is *not* addiction. A patient with a physiological dependence can quit the drug, usually by being tapered off it gradually, with medical supervision and without admission into a drug treatment program.

Prescription Drug Abuse Checklist

Ask yourself the following questions about opioids, sedatives, and stimulants:

- Have you been taking sleeping pills every day for more than three months?
- Do you sometimes take pills in order to make life more bearable?
- Have you tried to stop taking pills and felt vulnerable or frightened?
- Have you tried to stop taking pills and felt your body start to tremble or shake?
- Do you continue to take pills even though the medical reason for taking them is no longer present?
- Do you think pills are more important than family and friends?
- Are you mixing pills with wine, liquor, or beer?
- Are you taking one kind of pill to combat the effects of another pill?
- Do you take pills to get high and have fun?
- Do you take pills when you're upset or to combat loneliness?

- Do you feel happy if your doctor writes a prescription for drugs that change your mood?
- Do you visit several doctors to get the same prescription?
- Are you taking more pills to achieve the same effect you used to experience with smaller doses?
- Do you find it difficult to fulfill work obligations when you're taking pills?
- Do you ever promise yourself that you will stop taking pills, and then break the promise?
- If you answer yes or *sometimes* to three or more of these questions, you may be developing a problem with drug dependence. Talk with a chemical dependency counselor or doctor who specializes in treating drug problems. For referral to a local resource, call 1-800-NCA-CALL (1-800-622-2255).

Reprinted with permission from the Women's Alcohol and Drug Education Project, Women's Action Alliance, Inc.

2

Voices of Recovery

Millions of Americans are in recovery from addictive diseases. Still, if you are stuck in the addiction trap, you may be like many others who believe deeply that recovery is impossible for you—you *know* you cannot live without drugs. Recovery may work for others, but you're convinced it won't work for you. Among those who are struggling with addiction, this is a common belief. Common...but untrue.

In this chapter, you'll hear the stories of individuals in recovery from addiction to prescription drugs. Some of them underwent serious ordeals that nearly cost them their lives. In most of these stories, you'll note the individuals were "unwitting" addicts. They had not abused drugs previously, but began using the drugs for legitimate reasons. When the medications relieved their emotional pain, they started to abuse the drugs and were gradually pulled into the "vortex" of addiction. As several individuals explain, they were slow to realize that their therapeutic use of medication had escalated to addiction.

Listen carefully to their voices. Their message is clear: Recovery is possible. A better, richer life is possible.

Joan, 42
Software Specialist

My five-year addiction involved the drug hydrocodone—Vicodin. When it all started, I was working for a large high-tech company and also had been a fitness trainer for about twenty years. I was divorced with three small children. I started dating a man, Mark, who was a deputy sheriff; he introduced me to Vicodin. He was on disability from an accident, so he could get painkillers pretty easily. In hindsight, I realize he was addicted, but I started taking a pill with him now and then in the evenings. I considered it recreational—like having a glass of wine to relax. As my life as a single mother became more stressful, I started relying on the Vicodin more and more. Sometimes if Mark was getting low on drugs, I would go to urgent care and complain of pain from a past knee surgery. Between the two of us, we could always get painkillers.

The pills dulled my senses, but they gave me a ton of energy. I could work full time, take care of the kids, clean the house, and I felt happy and relaxed. The drugs gave me a warm feeling inside, and I just didn't feel stressed. I was learning to really like the feelings my drugs gave me, and I had no realization that they were highly addictive.

If I took too many of the pills, I would get very groggy and my speech would slur. At times I would fall asleep sitting up. It was around this time that Mark went to his orthopedic surgeon and got Soma, a muscle relaxant. His surgeon told him to be very careful about taking the Soma and hydrocodone—that they could be a very potent cocktail. Still, we were both eager to try it. The combination of drugs did give us a great high—we were very euphoric. As time went on, I would take two and a half tablets of Vicodin and three tablets of Soma. Then, within two hours, I would take another dose because the medication would be wearing off.

I hid my addiction most of the time, but there were times I would be at work and would be really loopy. People knew something was wrong. I would just tell them that I hadn't slept and that I was really stressed. I lost about twenty pounds. I stand five feet eleven inches tall, and I was down to 120 pounds. The drugs took away my appetite. At one point, I went into a seizure—I couldn't stand up or talk. I was taken to urgent care a couple of times and even admitted to the hospital once. I'm lucky I didn't lose my job.

As I mentioned, this went on for about five years. Then, a year and a half ago, Mark died of an accidental overdose. He was only forty. We were in the process of breaking up, but I still cared about him. This death was a real shock. It was also a wake-up call—I realized the drugs killed him. So, I cut back on taking the drugs for about two weeks, but I was so miserable with the withdrawal and depressed about losing Mark, I wanted to numb the pain. So, I started taking painkillers again.

My habit was costing me about $1,200 a month. I was borrowing money from my parents to pay rent, but I didn't care as long as I had money to buy drugs. I even stole Vicodin from my dad; he had it for back pain. I knew that I was addicted, but I could not stop.

Then, about a year ago, I was about to run out of pills. Finally, I was so very tired of all the lies I was telling. I didn't have the energy to go back to urgent care and lie. I was worried about stopping the pills, but I was also ashamed and guilt-ridden. I also realized I was putting my kids at risk. They were ages twelve, nine, and seven. There were a couple of times that I blacked out while driving with them in the car. One time, I managed to pull off the road before I blacked out. When I came to, my kids were scared and crying. They were using a cell phone, trying to call for help.

I was a terrible mother during this time. I lay around all the time. I didn't participate in activities with them. I was affectionate with them and never abusive, but I was simply absent emotionally. I'm still trying to make this up to them, because I was not there for them during key years of their lives.

I went off the drugs cold turkey, which is not recommended by the experts. The withdrawal was horrible. I was nauseated. I had chills and severe diarrhea. I had headaches and the shakes. But I still managed to go to work. I would sit in front of my computer with my head in my hands and just tremble. I lived from one minute to the next. Finally, after about six days I started feeling a little better. I called my sister a lot; she's been in recovery from alcoholism for twenty years. She was a good support. As I started to feel better, I realized I did not want to take pills again, because I never, ever wanted to go through withdrawal again.

I started going to Narcotics Anonymous meetings. When I first went, I thought that I had nothing in common with the people there. Some were on parole. Others had lost their driver's license. Some were poorly dressed and unkempt. Still, I went to meetings every day during my lunch hour. I was desperate for help. The more I listened, the more I realized I was like these people. We had different outsides, but had the same stories inside. I remember one man there—he held my hand and listened to me. He'd call me daily to check on me.

One time, after I started attending other support meetings, I walked into a session and saw a woman I knew from work. I always thought she had it all together. She was always well dressed and very professional. I always thought she had life by the tail. When we saw each other, we hugged. At the next meeting, she told her story. She had been on crack and heroin for five years before getting into recovery.

As I look back now, I think I took drugs because I had low self-esteem. Since adolescence, I had not felt really good about myself. The drugs filled the void…for a while.

Turning Point: My turning point really came when I started to run out of drugs and realized how exhausted I was from the years of lying and deceiving people to get pills.

Advice to Others: Get support. Don't try to recover by yourself. Go to support meetings such as Narcotics Anonymous. It was so comforting to me to know that I wasn't the only one who had this problem. Talking about my addiction at meetings helped me get rid of some of the shame and guilt that I had carried for years. That shame really kept me tied to my addiction.

Jeff, 31

Salesman

I used drugs recreationally in high school...marijuana, cocaine, and acid. I took my first painkiller when I was eighteen. I became addicted and continued to take prescription painkillers, such as Vicodin and OxyContin, for the next twelve years. My life revolved around my drugs. I would take fifteen to twenty pills a day just to feel normal. I have been in recovery now for about a year.

Why was I taking these drugs? In hindsight, I realize now that I felt empty inside. I wasn't really happy with myself. Drugs numbed the pain. In high school, I was an all-state athlete. Other people thought I had a lot going for me, but it was never enough for me.

Once out of high school, I sold drugs to make money. I could not hold down a job. I would steal money and manipulate people in order to support my habit. I stole money from friends, drug dealers, my parents, my girlfriend. Finally, at twenty-two, I had burned so many bridges with people who cared about me that I moved East to live with my aunt. There, I stopped taking drugs. I went through bad withdrawals, and I didn't leave the house for almost two weeks. But then I started feeling better. It was the first time in a long time that I started thinking I could live life without drugs. I even went to a couple of AA meetings.

I was probably off drugs for about two months. Then, a couple of my old friends came to visit me for New Year's. They brought Vicodin, so I took some. But by that time, I had gotten a job and a promotion into management, and I realized that the drugs were going to hurt me. So, I stopped taking any drugs...for a while.

About a year later, I took another management job and was sent back to my hometown area for training. Being back in that environment was a huge trigger for me to start using again. The minute I walked into my parents' house, I went into their bathroom and looked in their medicine cabinet. There was a bottle of Percocets. I took about half of them with me. My drug use escalated. Soon, I was snorting OxyContin and my addiction was full blown again. However, I was what I would call a "functioning addict." I could go to work and appear normal. Others would not have known I was addicted to OxyContin. I met my girlfriend during this time, and got married. I told her early on that I had had a drug problem, but she didn't know much about addiction. It was a while before she realized that I still had a problem.

It costs a lot of money to support an OxyContin habit. I spent about $500 every time I made a buy. Over the years, I probably spent $100,000 on OxyContin and other drugs. Through my job, I knew people who could connect me with someone I could buy drugs from. Once, I stole drugs from my wife's mother. She realized it and knew it was me. I went to her and apologized. She was crying. I felt pretty low.

I also lost a job because of my drug use. I then got other jobs, where I could steal money to buy drugs. Over a period of a few years, I probably stole more than $25,000. I lived every day worried that I would get a knock on my door, and it would be the police there to arrest me.

I wanted to get off drugs, but I couldn't help myself. By this time, my wife had given birth to our son, and I really wanted to be a good father. But I could not stop the drugs even though I knew they were going to kill me eventually. I know I came close to overdosing more than once. There would be times in the night when my wife would shake me awake because my breathing would be slowed down by the drugs I had taken.

My relationship with my wife was becoming troubled. She was exasperated with me and my drug use. One time, my dad gave me $1,400 to buy new carpet before the baby was born. I spent the money on drugs. More than once, my wife and my parents begged me to get help. One day, I simply agreed with them. I made arrangements to go to a treatment center. Before I went, I called all the friends and people who I had gotten drugs from. I told them I was going into a detox and treatment center and begged them to never sell me drugs and to not even take my call if I called them in the future.

I stayed at the treatment center for two weeks. The treatment did help me. I had supervised detox, and I went to a lot of group counseling sessions. I had a lot of guilt and shame over all the things I had done in the past. However, I could not sleep well during the two weeks I was there. When my wife and little boy came to visit, I felt terrible that they had to come there to see me. It was painful when they left. Two days before I was to be discharged, I left.

The cab driver who drove me home asked me why I had been at the treatment center, so I told him. He then told me his story of having been an addict for seventeen years before getting sober. It was ironic that I was hearing his story. It was like a reminder for me to get more help. The next day, I went to a support group. I raised my hand to talk. I told them I had just left rehab and that I needed help. That was the day I got my sponsor. I've continued going to meetings for the last four years. Narcotics Anonymous has saved my life. Everyone there has the same problem. And we all have the same goal.

I have had two relapses since then. It hasn't been easy. I have struggled daily. Before the relapses, I believed about half of what I heard in support meetings. Now, after two relapses, I listen to what people tell me in those meetings. I don't dismiss what I hear as something that doesn't pertain to me. I'm off drugs now because I've stayed out of my own way.

Turning Point: When my wife and my parents confronted me about getting help. I just didn't want to argue with them anymore. Deep down I knew I had a serious problem. I told them that I thought they were right, that I needed help. I really didn't want to use drugs anymore. I had a family, and I wanted to be a good parent. Then, I think an even bigger turning point came when I started participating in support meetings—opening up, talking, and not holding in all my emotions. I had come to realize that recovery was not going to happen just by osmosis. I needed to do the work emotionally.

Advice to Others: Go to a support group. Stay off drugs one day at a time. You don't have to worry about the month ahead or the rest of your life. Just worry about today.

Gary, 40

Businessman

Looking back, I realize I am an alcoholic, but I had never let my drinking get out of control until 1999. I had begun drinking more then because I was under a lot of stress with my work—I owned several companies. I was also married and had three small children. Still, I managed to exercise rigorously; I'm a runner.

I started working out with a personal trainer at my gym. As we got to know each other, I told him that I was over-extended and stressed a great deal of the time. He took me into his office and said, "I've got something that can help you." He handed me a pill. I asked him what it was and whether it had any side effects. I had never abused pills before. He told me it was just a pain pill, that he and his brother-in-law had taken them for a couple of years with no problem. So, I took one—20 milligrams, the size of an aspirin. The pill was OxyContin, which I had never heard of. It is a very strong pain medication that also has a very high potential for addiction. My descent into pure hell was about to begin.

In the beginning, the drug was absolutely wonderful. It was the answer to all my problems. I felt euphoric. I felt in control. And strangely, I felt organized. I could handle all my business and family matters. I could handle the world, I thought. I bought about thirty pills for about $10 apiece. They lasted about ten days. I was taking two or more pills a day.

Then I ran out of pills. I started feeling so bad, I couldn't get out of bed. I thought I had a severe case of the flu. My muscles ached. I didn't realize it at the time, but I was going through withdrawal. I talked to my trainer from the gym, who told me I was in withdrawal and that I needed more drugs. So, I bought some more—anything to get over feeling so sick. When I bought the second batch from him, it was the first time I knew what they were called. He called them "Oxys." I realized that I was addicted already. I took a pill and felt better almost immediately. My wife thought I had a twenty-four-hour flu.

Three months later, I was still taking the Oxys. But I was training for a marathon, a twenty-six-mile race, and I was having trouble—my muscles kept aching. So, I took more pills. Although I wasn't feeling euphoric anymore, like I did in the beginning, I was having to take the pills just to keep from getting sick. My tolerance went through the roof so quickly. By now, I was taking about twenty pills a day. I was still seeking the "buzz" I had gotten the first time I took them. I had learned I could get a faster "fix" by chewing the pills or crushing them and then snorting them.

The day of the marathon, I had pills in my running shorts. I knew I would need them. But thirteen miles into the race, I could not make it. I walked and shuffled through the last thirteen miles. Once I got into the runners' tent, I was a mess. Everyone thought I was having heat exhaustion. In reality, I was needing more drugs, even though I had taken forty that day.

About a month later, I was such a mess, I finally told my wife that I was addicted to OxyContin. She called the police and reported the trainer. It turns out he was a dealer who had gotten four other people addicted. He was getting the drug from a crooked doctor, who was arrested and barred from practicing.

My wife was supportive, and I decided to go into treatment. I went into a rehab hospital, where I was undergoing detox, but I stayed only eight days. I didn't think I needed treatment, and I wanted to go on vacation with my family. But very soon I started feeling sick again. Not only my muscles ached, but it felt like even my bones ached. Amazingly, I stuck it out, and in a few weeks, I was feeling better again. I stayed off OxyContin…for a while.

About a year later, I was under a great deal of pressure. I had made a huge business purchase and was a couple of million dollars in debt. Believe it or not, I called the guy who had gotten me hooked the first time. Within five minutes he was at my office with more OxyContin. I began using the drug again.

I really believed I could use the pills just a little, as I needed them. But within two weeks, I was back up to twenty pills a day, and they were costing me $20 a pill, twice the price I first paid. After several months, I broke down and told my wife I was using Oxys again.

I went into another treatment center, and they kept me for only three days (in detox), then told me to go home and continue as an outpatient. Within an hour of leaving the facility, I was going through withdrawal. I had the "skin crawls," which felt like bugs crawling all over me. Within two days, I was using Oxys again.

Sadly, over the next six months, I got clean and then relapsed three times before I finally decided to get serious about treatment. Each time, all it took was one pill. One pill and I was a full-fledged addict. And each time, I would lie to my wife about using the drug. Finally, she purchased a home-testing kit for opiate use and made me take a drug test. When she saw that I was not giving up the drug, she started going to Al-Anon meetings and gave me an ultimatum: Get clean or get out.

Turning Point: When my wife gave me the ultimatum. I knew I would lose my children. Plus, I was so miserable. I recall holding my baby boy in my arms and snorting OxyContin. I just started crying. I couldn't stand to look at myself in the mirror. I had been a successful businessman, had run marathons, and had a wonderful wife and kids. Now, I was so disgusted with what I had done to my life. Finally, I wanted to get better. I wanted treatment.

Advice to Others: If you are in the shape I was in, realize you need some long-term treatment. It *will* help you. Also, after treatment, get into a support group such as Narcotics Anonymous or AA. Don't try to do it alone. Link up with others in recovery who have gone through the same kind of ordeal. This kind of support is critical. And remember, the general public doesn't understand addiction. They just think you should stop being a "scumbag" and stop using drugs. If only it were that easy. They don't understand it is a disease and some of us will have to be vigilant about staying in recovery all our lives.

Jeana, 29

Public Relations Director

I went to a Christian school. I never did drugs. I don't even drink. My ordeal with addiction came about as a result of chronic pain, which started when I was diagnosed with Crohn's disease at age seventeen. It's a chronic intestinal disorder that causes abdominal pain, cramping, fatigue, and diarrhea. The only treatment for me was surgery—I had to have my entire large bowel removed. I received an ileostomy, the surgical construction of a connection from the small bowel to the abdomen, which allows for the discharge of bodily waste.

I had abdominal pain, a lot of pain. So I was prescribed painkillers, Tylenol with Codeine and Percocet, which soon became my drug of choice. I didn't let anyone know that I was taking more than what was prescribed. By the time I was twenty, I was an addict. I abused drugs for seven long years. I thought I needed these medications to function normally.

At one point, I moved to the Cleveland area and found out my new physician was not as liberal in prescribing narcotics, so I began doctor shopping and making numerous visits to local emergency rooms. It was such a hassle to make doctor appointments and it was expensive, so I began writing my own prescriptions. On a visit to a doctor's office, I had noticed a black-and-white prescription pad on the desk. I figured the only other things I needed were his DEA (Drug Enforcement Administration) number, a bottle of Liquid Paper, a black pen, and a copying machine and I was in business.

I started off writing a script for thirty pills and moved my way up to ninety. I visited every pharmacy in town. It worked for about a month. And then I got caught. I remember the day. I had forgotten I had visited a particular pharmacy three days earlier, and the pharmacist became suspicious. He called the doctor to verify the script and found it was fraudulent. He told me I was never to step foot in his pharmacy again. It scared me, but I was thankful I had gotten away with it...or so I thought. The next Saturday afternoon, about three days after my "incident" at the pharmacy, I received a phone call. I checked the caller ID and noticed the call was from a county office. My first thought was that I didn't have any overdue books, so why would the county library be calling?

I answered the phone only to find a detective from the county sheriff's department on the other end of the line. As he was introducing himself, I was wracking my brain to come up with a good lie about the forged prescriptions. But somehow I knew he knew. I offered to go to his office immediately, but he suggested we wait until Wednesday. I thought, "Oh my God, I have to live with this up in the air for four long days?" I didn't know who to tell, if anyone. Finally, on Tuesday night, I broke down and called my aunt, who's always been more like a sister to me. I begged her to accompany me.

We met the detective at his office. It was a cold February day. He took my aunt and me into his office. We introduced ourselves, and before I could say anything else, he was reading me my rights. I just started crying. I thought this couldn't be real. Oh, but it was very real. My aunt began to explain that my family was well aware I had a severe problem and that my Crohn's disease was the true cause for my addiction. He explained he needed to meet with his captain and the prosecutor to discuss what they were going to do. We were then escorted to the captain's office and were told what the legal repercussions were for what I had done. I could face twenty-four years in prison. Finally, they told me that given my health problems they would let me go, but warned if I ever repeated such a crime, I would be charged for all the scripts I forged. Still, I didn't get sober right away. That would take time.

I went through rehab a total of four times in a nine-month period, but each time I came out of rehab and went back to using. In hindsight, I think I looked at treatment as a cure—I would check in and the good doctors would fix me. I wasn't aware of the fact that recovery was something I had to do. The detoxification process each time went fairly smoothly. I always completed each aftercare program yet still couldn't suppress my overwhelming craving to self-medicate.

By now, I was at the peak of my addiction, and had developed a huge tolerance for my drugs. I was taking between fifty and sixty Percocets per day. I would do just about anything to obtain a prescription. I liked the idea of sobriety, but I loved the high more. In fact, I cared about my drugs more than my marriage—I was divorced from my husband of two years. And I literally robbed family members of money and even raided their medicine cabinets for anything with a drowsiness sticker on the label. I stole money from my grandmother. I broke into our family business, stealing the cash box and credit cards. I had no boundaries. I was numb. I was eventually banned from all my family members' homes and lives.

I had nowhere to go, so I decided to run away to Florida. I was all alone. My family had always been there to pick up the pieces when I lived in Ohio. But now they refused to help me, financially or otherwise. I was holding down a job as a waitress in a casino, but I was still using. My life was terrible. I was penniless and had no transportation. I couldn't break the cycle of abuse. I was too busy feeling sorry for myself and beating myself up for the mistakes I had made. I had dropped out of school, lost my marriage, friends, and family. And most importantly, I had lost myself.

I had hit bottom. I wanted a better life. I began doing some reading about addiction and realized that I wasn't so alone or so crazy. That same year, my parents sent me a home Bible study for Christmas. I began doing a lesson every night. I was realizing that no matter how bad things had gotten, I could at least try to make tomorrow better than today. I guess you could say I had a moment of clarity. If I had truly learned from the mistakes I had made, I wouldn't make them again. I remember talking myself out of numerous doctor appointments where I had planned to get more drugs. Sometimes, I was taking life minute by minute.

I realized I had to put into practice what I learned in rehab. It broke my heart to realize that one of the few memories I had of my mother was with tears in her eyes, asking, "Where is that little girl I raised?" I didn't know. I didn't remember that girl. How could I find her again? I just wanted to be me. I wanted to be happy. I wanted to feel again. I had to take control of my life. I had to live up to my word to myself. I clung to my sobriety knowing no one could take it away from me. I knew how hard it was just to stay off the drugs. If I could stay sober, I knew I could do just about anything. Inside I knew I was a survivor of my own war, the fight for my life and soul.

I had been clean for about a month when I took a big step and moved back to my hometown. Getting off the drugs was hard, but so was accepting responsibility for my actions and making amends with others. I approached each of my family members individually and apologized for my actions. I had to accept responsibility no matter how painful it was. Being around my family was uneasy for months.

I realize now that during those three years I spent trying to get myself together, they had been hurting, too. They felt as though they had failed me in some way when in reality I had been the selfish one. I didn't have answers to all their questions. I had to accept that I was an addict. I didn't know why I had chosen this for myself. I had to show them that this time I was really dedicated to making my life right. I remember a friend telling me he could tell I wasn't on drugs anymore because I actually had a personality again. Someone could really tell the difference. Finally! I began to reap the rewards of sobriety. That's when I knew I wanted to be clean and stay clean. I no longer had to worry about getting drugs and getting caught. I no longer had to look over my shoulder. I was truly free.

I am proud to say I have been sober for three years now. My relationship with my family is better than it has ever been. My mother and I speak to groups to help others who are struggling with addiction. We have made it our mission to shed the social stigmas of addiction. We are neither the first family nor the last to suffer this pain. I attribute my successful recovery to the fact that I really wanted it. I also had faith in God and I always knew my family loved me. I had to learn to love myself despite the consequences of my past.

Ironically, I learned during a visit to a pain clinic that the drugs I was taking were actually the reason for my discomfort. Percocet and other opiates actually immobilize the bowel at times, causing pain. I did not need the drugs to treat my original abdominal pain. I needed them to feed my addiction.

A gift that has come from my recovery is my continued relationship with the detective who arrested me. He became one of my biggest supporters and still is. When I would call the detective, he never judged me or questioned me. He just listened. His support meant so much to me because he was a stranger—he didn't have to like me. He seemed to actually empathize with my pain but didn't buy into my feeble excuses.

Turning Point: When I was in Florida all alone and realized that my life was a mess and I was the only one who could change it.

Advice to Others: Forgive yourself. Know that you are not alone. Understand that recovery takes complete dedication. Take each day second by second if you have to. There is comfort knowing that it is never too late. Quit trying to look back. Focus on your future. The only feelings you can change are your own. No one can change the past, but the future is yours. If you fall down, pick yourself up and try again until you get it right. The hunger for pills can be overwhelming—it was all I could do not to run to the nearest ER and dupe some doctor into giving me what I wanted. The rewards of sobriety are endless. There is power in knowing deep down inside you can be accountable for your actions. Stop excusing your behavior and change it. Work on learning to be a respectable and trustworthy person again. Treat sobriety as something that is more valuable than all the riches in the world. No longer mourn for the person you once were or the innocence you have lost. Celebrate the person you are.

Margaret, 25

Homemaker

I knew nothing about prescription drug abuse. I'd never done any sort of drugs. But several years ago, I broke my arm and was given Vicodin for pain. I ended up going through a drug ordeal for about a year and a half. The Vicodin made me feel better—sort of a euphoria. I kept going back to the doctor and getting prescriptions for a hundred Vicodin with refills. No one told me the drug was addictive.

By the time my arm was getting better, I stopped taking the medication. But I would get really sick and would go to the emergency room with migraines. I never equated the drug with my headaches. At the emergency room, I would be given Vicodin. The headache would go away. I figured I had a migraine problem, so I continued the Vicodin for the headaches. I later realized that the headaches were from withdrawal from the drug.

Without the drug, within twenty-four hours I would have these really bad headaches again. I would try aspirin, but then I would start craving Vicodin. It was an addiction, a vicious circle. Then, once the drug had a hold on me, I wasn't living life on life's terms. Anytime something upset me, it would be an excuse to take more medication. I could forget about my problems much like an alcoholic would with liquor.

Because of my managed health-care plan, when I went to the doctor I rarely saw the same doctor. My addiction went undetected. When I finally did see my own doctor, he told me I had a dependency problem. I'd been taking Vicodin for a year and a half, and it was only toward the end of this time that I realized that the pills, not the headaches, were my problem.

Then I had to go through a drug detox. It was an outpatient program; I had two kids to take care of. I was given other medications to help ease the discomfort. But, for about seven days, I stayed in my bedroom—I couldn't function at all. I couldn't sleep. I had memory problems. I was exhausted. I had no energy to do anything.

For about four months, I went to personal counseling, to AA meetings, and to a prescription drug abuse class. Every day was a struggle. I had to learn how to live life all over again. I am still afraid of relapsing. I'm horrified of ever having an injury or surgery for which I might need pain medication. I think what really upsets me is that I was never warned that I was getting a highly addictive drug. I didn't have a clue.

Turning Point: was tired of being sick. Through groups and treatment, I learned to make myself feel better in different ways. I started exercising a lot. I jogged and walked. I bought a StairMaster. It made me feel a lot better. I started focusing on me, taking care of my emotional needs.

Advice to Others: There is light at the end of the tunnel. It may take a while, but hang in there.

Bill, 72

Physician

I was about twenty-seven, in my residency training for medical school, when I had a painful kidney stone attack. I was given an injection of codeine. Never in all my life had I felt the feeling that drug gave me. The euphoria was just incredible. I stored that in my memory bank, and then every time I had a kidney stone attack—and I had many—I would ask for a shot of codeine. Then the kidney stone attacks subsided, and I was getting on with my life and my medical practice.

Later, in my forties, I had a series of health problems and had to have several surgeries—for a lumbar disk, cervical disk, my knee, and later my right hip. I would be given painkillers after each surgery, and I would extend my usage of the drugs. I managed to always con the doctors into giving me a little extra. Gradually, I increased my use of the drugs and became a full-fledged addict.

During a ten-year period, two of my drugs of choice were Dilaudid and Demerol—both powerful painkillers. I never prescribed for myself since that was illegal, but I used samples from drug companies. I also received drugs from those who'd had a death in the family; they would call me and ask me what to do with pain medications after their loved ones died. I would tell them to drop off the drugs at my office. It's pathetic, but true.

At one point, I was also injecting drugs. I had read that in times of emergency, one could inject a patient through the clothing without having to get the patient undressed. That's all I needed to read. I began injecting myself through my clothing. It was quicker, more convenient. As a result, I would often have blood on my pants or lab coat when I was in the office. Every time someone said, "Oh, there's blood on you," I'd say, "Oh, I must have spilled some blood in the lab."

Looking back, I was crying for help and nobody heard me. I was hooked. I had to have drugs. As with most addicts, I no longer got the rush from the drugs, like I did early on. I needed the drugs to maintain, to keep from getting sick.

Eventually, as a result of injecting myself through clothing, I got a serious blood infection. When my physician asked me about the infection, I told him I had been injecting myself for pain. Even then, I really didn't consider myself an addict. I was still in deep denial.

During the course of the years I was addicted, I destroyed many relationships—both personal and in business. Thankfully, I managed to do no harm in my medical practice.

Turning Point: I got into trouble with the law. I was busted by two undercover narcotic agents who came to my office because they noticed my excessive prescribing for other patients. I had prescribed Valium for two undercover agents. Arrested as I was coming back from lunch, I was handcuffed and paraded through my office full of patients and put in jail. The arrest saved my life. I got into treatment in 1997. Since then, I've worked the twelve steps of recovery in AA, and have reached out to be of service to other people.

Advice to Others: Get to a physician who specializes in addiction. That's number one—find a doctor who understands what you're going through. Also, recognize that you are powerless over the world around you—powerless over people and places. This is the first of the twelve steps of recovery. You have to realize that you cannot control everything in your life. Only then can you regain control of your life. It's also important to realize that your anger, fears, and shame are all generated by your own brain. Recovery can help you cope with these.

Michelle, 31

Businesswoman

I had no experience with drugs—illegal or legal. I'd never even heard of most of the prescriptions I ended up taking. After graduating from college, I started working for a large corporation. I got promoted to the position of computer system specialist. I was young and had a lot of responsibility, including oversight of thirty-seven sales reps and their budgets. I liked it, but it was more pressure than I was used to.

I started getting really bad headaches and went to my doctor. At the first appointment, the doctor prescribed Fiorinal, which I later learned is a narcotic. Within a few weeks, my headaches were continuing, and so I started getting injections of Demerol, which I had never heard of. I had a standing prescription to go into the doctor's office and have the nurse give me a shot of Demerol. I know now that it is a Schedule II narcotic like morphine.

Soon, however, I was having the headaches daily. I'd have worse headaches if I didn't get the injections. But I was really getting worse and worse headaches. My family started getting very worried about me. We all knew something was very wrong. I would wake up in the morning shaking and vomiting. I didn't realize I was having withdrawal from the Demerol.

My family had never been around drug users, so we didn't know that my symptoms were actually drug withdrawal. The doctors were writing down my symptoms, but no one seemed to suspect drug withdrawal from an opiate. Often, I got the shots from nurses and never saw a doctor. I still didn't connect the medication with what I thought was an illness. I was getting sicker and sicker and the medication wasn't helping. So my family insisted that I be hospitalized for tests. During that hospital stay, I was on an IV, and I was to the point by now of ordering the Demerol myself. I knew just exactly what I needed in order to feel better. I'd tell the nurses, "I need 100 milligrams of Demerol every two to three hours." And they would give it to me.

A year earlier, I'd never even heard of Demerol and now I knew how to order it. I was asking for it IM (intramuscularly) or IV (intravenously) with Vistaril or with Phenergan. Vistaril, a sedative, acted like a "kicker" and made the Demerol last longer. Phenergan was an antinausea drug. I knew just exactly what I wanted.

Then, within a three-day period, I'd had over a gram of Demerol, and I had a grand mal seizure. I remember waking up with two doctors and a nurse in the room with me. I had blood in my mouth and all over my shirt. They told me I had seized.

I was never diagnosed with any illness. My problem was Demerol. So from there I had to go into chemical dependence recovery. My family put me in a care unit. There, at first, I thought I was completely out of place. I was with addicts who were talking about "highballs" and "eight balls," things I had no knowledge of. My attitude was that I just needed to get my life back on track and be done with doctors and drugs, but that was not the case. My doctor in the care unit said I was the worst case of detox he'd seen from legal or illegal drugs. I was in detox seven days longer than some of the heroin addicts.

My denial was really high, because I didn't think I was truly an addict. I just thought my other doctors had put me on too much medication. But I had to finally say, "I'm responsible for my recovery, and regardless of how I got here, I'm here." Being angry didn't really help me.

Demerol is like heroin. It's very hard to stop taking. I did finish my inpatient treatment and then started going to support groups. But I still felt out of place; I didn't think these meetings were what I needed. A lot of prescription drug addicts feel out of place in twelve-step meetings. In Narcotics Anonymous they were talking about illegal drugs and at AA meetings they were talking about alcohol, so I had a hard time fitting in. That just fed my denial. I could say, "None of this fits for me." I heard only the differences, not the similarities.

Twelve-Step Programs

The "twelve-steps" are the guiding principles of many support groups; the steps were originally established by Alcoholics Anonymous. As summarized by the American Psychological Association, twelve-step programs involve the following:

- Admitting that one cannot control one's addiction or compulsion
- Recognizing a greater power that can give strength
- Examining past errors with the help of a sponsor (experienced member)
- Making amends for these errors
- Learning to live a new life with a new code of behavior
- Helping others who suffer from the same addictions or compulsions

So I went back to work, against my doctor's advice. He told me, "Your problem is no longer headaches—your problem is about surviving. People die from this." He really wanted me to have more recovery.

But I went back to work and went out one night with friends and had a few drinks. I'd never had a drinking problem so I didn't think there was any danger. But within hours of taking a couple of drinks, my craving for Demerol was back. I relapsed. That's how quickly it happened.

I felt really hopeless then. In AA you hear people talking about hitting the "bottom bottom," when you feel like you can't live with the drugs but you can't live without them. I hated the way I was living. I opted to keep taking the drugs and to make myself be happy. I went to the Caribbean on vacation and tried to tell myself I was okay. But it didn't take me long to end up feeling really hopeless. I knew I couldn't go on that way.

So then I was hospitalized two or three times in psych wards; my family intervened—they wanted to help. Yet, I was angry and yelled at them. It seemed like everything that had been important to me in life was no longer important. The only thing that mattered was not feeling sick from the drugs but at the same time wanting them so I could feel normal. That was all that mattered. I was angry and bitter about everything.

Turning Point: I took two bottles of pills—a suicide attempt. I woke up in a medical center. And maybe it was grace from above, but somehow when I woke up, I felt like maybe I could get help. I remembered meeting people in support groups who, like me, had been in trouble with prescription drugs. I had a bit of hope. I thought I could return to the twelve-step groups for help. I started going back to AA meetings and Narcotics Anonymous.

Advice to Others: I came to realize that I was worth getting better. And every single person in that situation is. I held onto that. I found help in twelve-step meetings. I found help in dealing with all my resentments about what had happened to me. I had a lot of guilt and shame, too. The support groups helped me find a way to deal with that and learn to take better care of myself. I had a supportive family, but still I had to do the work. They couldn't do it for me. I suggest reaching out to people. Learn to trust others.

Justin, 37

Attorney

I dislocated my shoulder and broke my wrist by falling down a set of stairs. It affected the nerves that ran into my neck, head, and jaw, so I had intense pain. That gave me my first exposure to pain medication.

After a while, I told the doctor that my medication, Codeine No. 3, was not stopping the pain. He said to take two. After a couple of months, when the pain persisted, my doctor gave me Codeine No. 4, which was twice the strength of the No. 3. So I was getting 120 milligrams per dose, prescribed for four hours apart. I would use the medication as needed, but was gradually using it more and more. Dependency was kicking in. My tolerance was building, and I really didn't realize how much I was using it. It was a very gradual thing. It never occurred to me that I had a drug problem.

Two years, later my jaw pain continued, so I went to a different medical center for tests and X-rays. I was told I had a problem with my jaw and needed surgery. However, my insurance plan would not pay for it. So my doctors said we could only treat the pain. I told my physician that I thought I was dependent on the codeine. I knew I had built up a tolerance and if I didn't take the medication, I would feel sick. I was afraid that I was becoming dependent. My doctor said it's not unusual to need ongoing medication for pain management, so I was sent to a special department for treatment. There, I was given Vicodin, which was more potent than what I was taking.

Within a couple of weeks, I was really needing the drug. Every time I went back to see my doctor, I would tell him I needed more pills. So I would get more. Then, I was switched to Percocet and would get occasional shots of Demerol or morphine suppositories. I also had muscle relaxants and tranquilizers.

With the opiate drugs, you build a tolerance, so other people don't readily notice you're on a drug. You just need it to keep from getting sick. However, I now realize my behavior was changing. I wasn't dealing with life normally. I would be jubilant sometimes, deeply depressed other times. My motivation to do things was affected. I managed to adjust my dosages so I could function at work, but I did call in sick a lot. I was having problems in my marriage—we eventually got divorced. I had no idea my problems were related to drug use. I just thought I was suffering from depression.

A couple of years later, I overdosed. I had received a shot of Demerol and came home and took tranquilizers. I went to sleep and woke up and took more tranquilizers. I was never really aware of how many pills I was taking. It is quite common, once your judgment is impaired, to not realize how many more pills you're taking. That same night, when I started to take even more pills, I did realize the bottle of 100 tablets was nearly empty. I got really scared. I knew I was not feeling right. I called 911. When the ambulance got there, I was delirious. I ended up in the intensive care unit and almost died.

Once I got out of the hospital, I got my prescriptions refilled and started all over again. I knew the drugs were a problem, but every single day was a major effort for me to try to quit. I had to have the drugs. I would get 150 milligrams of Demerol in a shot and then take Percodan.

I was feeding a real drug habit now. I tried several times to get treatment and go through detox, but then I'd still have real physical pain in my neck. Finally, a few months later, I went to a specialist who performed surgery on my neck—fixed my physical problem—and that helped me get over my drug addiction. With treatment, I got my life together.

Looking back, it seems the medical community didn't want to take time to explain the nature of addictive drugs. Still, it's important that they prescribe painkillers when a patient needs them. I've seen that problem with my mother, who legitimately needed pain medication but couldn't get it because her doctors were too cautious. I've seen both extremes. There needs to be balance.

Turning Point: By the time I was taking drugs every day for three months in a row, I knew I was in trouble. At first I thought I could stop by myself, but I couldn't. When I realized I couldn't stop, I became more scared. But I was also afraid that I couldn't live without the drugs.

I fought that fear for a year before I finally went for inpatient treatment. I was in for thirty days. I relapsed several times. I went back to inpatient treatment seven times, ranging from five days to five weeks. To this day, seven years later, I still go to AA meetings two or three times a week.

Advice to Others: The first thing I would say is, realize you *can* live without the drugs. I had become 100 percent convinced that I could not live without them. I thought it was great that other people could recover, but I was so addicted that I thought there was no way in hell I could function without the drugs.

If someone is dependent, they may have to take a giant leap of faith and realize that they can live life without drugs. It takes some time, and it's good to join a support group of people who are going through the same thing. Pair up with someone who has used a similar drug—they'll know exactly what you've gone through. Stick with these people who have been through it, and recovery can work for you.

Terry, 37

Nurse

I'm a nurse who ended up taking drugs on the job. This kind of abuse is rampant in hospitals all over the country. A lot of nurses need help. In one of my support groups, seven out of thirteen of us are nurses. The medical profession is so intense. You're so afraid of doing something wrong. There's a lot of pressure on medical professionals, and we have access to drugs. We want to help others and do everything perfectly. That's a lot of pressure. We're only human.

My problem started when I was a nurse on a psychiatric ward. I was injured when an enraged patient attacked me. I suffered a neck injury, and I was prescribed Vicodin. Eventually, I had to have carpal tunnel surgery and a thumb fusion because of the injury. I was on Vicodin for two years.

I loved the drug. It was wonderful. Life was easier. My husband was abusive, but when I was on the drug, whatever he did or said didn't bother me as much.

I built up a tolerance to the drug. I started taking one every three or four hours, then I'd take two. After a while, I was taking twenty pills a day. Being a nurse, I knew this wasn't right. But no one knew I was taking so many pills. The only change in me was that my emotions had become really flat.

By now, I was working in a long-term care unit and I was taking the hospital's drugs myself, signing charts as if patients were receiving them. I was the charge nurse. I had the key to the narcotics cabinet. I'd just write on a patient's chart that they'd taken a certain medication, and I took it instead. The DEA requires that the drugs be recorded on a narcotics sheet, so I'd sign out the drugs to a patient. I'd write down some excuse, that the patient had a headache or back pain. Then I'd take the drugs. It was easy. This went on for a year and a half. No one ever knew.

Later, I worked in a doctor's office, where drug samples were available from drug salespeople. These samples were never registered, so no one knew I was taking them. Once again, I had the key to the drug cabinet. I was taking Vicodin, Xanax, Restoril, Ativan, and Tylenol with Codeine.

I knew I was an addict, but thought since I was a nurse, I could stop on my own. I really tried, but I couldn't. No way. Had I stopped cold, I would have had a seizure and maybe died.

Eventually, I was phoning pharmacies with my own prescriptions—100 Vicodin a week. I worked for six doctors, so I would use their names, say I was calling from their office and order a script for Terry. I used five or six pharmacies. It was easy.

I was always preoccupied with getting pills. Anytime I started to run out of drugs, I would panic. I kept track on my watch: Was it time to take a pill?

The end came when I got busted at work. One of the doctors caught on that I was calling different pharmacies. That was on a Friday. I was fired. I was so humiliated, really ashamed. I considered suicide, but having two children made me realize I couldn't do that. So I admitted I needed help. I didn't want the drugs, but my body did. I could not stop. I knew I was dying. I was anorexic. I was so thin I couldn't even sit on a chair because my bones were sticking out. I'd lost seventy-three pounds. I knew I was going to die. In my mind, death was the only way to be free of the addiction. In fact, when you're that addicted, the cells in your body turn to the drug as their food. You don't feel like you need regular food or anything else—just that drug. If you take the drug away, it's like starving yourself to death.

So, I called a patient from our office who I knew was in recovery. She knew exactly what I needed. By Monday, I was in drug treatment. I was in detox for fifteen days. The first couple of days were okay, because I was being given drugs, but then my doses were gradually reduced. I couldn't sleep. I would shake. Just remembering what the physical withdrawal was like would keep me from ever relapsing. I ached all over. Muscle cramps. Diarrhea. Vomiting. My body screamed for the pills.

Once I was through detox, I had to start dealing with the emotional issues that caused me to drug myself in the first place, and those issues were still there, staring me in the face. I fought the feelings like crazy because I'd been through a lot of abuse in my life and I just didn't want to feel any of the buried pain I was going to have to face. I made it, but I would not have made it without the rehab center. I wouldn't have made it at home. I would have relapsed. The first ninety days are not easy.

I was blessed with a wonderful sponsor in my support group. She told me life would get better and that I deserved it. I started to believe it, even though it took me a while because I had been abused much of my life. I do believe in God, and my faith helped me.

Once I got out of inpatient treatment, I was scared to death that I would relapse. I went to two or three meetings (both AA and Narcotics Anonymous) a day for the first ninety days. That's how I did it. AA had more people with more years of sobriety, plus the structure there was good for me. In Narcotics Anonymous, the people expressed a lot of love. I needed both. I had to reach out.

I can't believe how good I feel now. I would never have thought I could feel so happy inside. I look forward to life. I was even hired back at the doctor's office where I was fired. I still go through rough times, but when I do, I call my sponsor and I get to a meeting. I wish everyone could have the luxury of a support system like I have. All these people will help you, but you have to reach out. You do have to make that effort. You have to be willing.

Turning Point: Getting busted at work was definitely the turning point for me.

Advice to Others: Be totally honest with everyone—your friends, your therapist, and your family. Admit that your life is screwed up and that you need help. Realize you're not perfect. I found it's really neat being "not perfect." Realizing I was just another human took the weight of the world off my shoulders. Today I have freedom, love, and hope in my life. It's amazing. And it gets better every day.

Karen, 65

Retired

I've been in recovery from prescription drug addiction for several years. It's ironic—all the time that I was abusing painkillers, I was going to AA meetings because I am also an alcoholic in recovery. However, I have not had a drink in twenty-three years.

My problem with drugs started several years ago, when my father was diagnosed with lymphoma and was given a year to live. I spent that last year flying back and forth between Cleveland and my home in Florida to be with him. It was stressful. About that same time, I started having shoulder pain. I was diagnosed with rheumatoid arthritis. My doctor gave me Vicodin for the pain. For almost a year, I took the medication as directed. I kept thinking I could handle the use of the painkillers, but control slipped away from me.

Then, my father died. I didn't want to feel the grief, so I began taking more pills. I knew I was risking my sobriety, but I was in denial. I thought that if I kept going to AA meetings, I could stay in control.

Then, I met a man who swept me off my feet. It turned out he was an addict, and he always encouraged me to take more pain pills to stay ahead of the pain from the arthritis. So I did, and my appetite for Vicodin increased. Finally, the addiction consumed me. I was getting the drug from several doctors.

My relationship with the man continued for several years before it fell apart and he left. But even though the relationship was not good for me, I didn't want to be alone. I took pills to ease my emotional pain.

I was seeing a therapist at the time, and one day, he asked me how many Vicodin I had taken that day. I told him it was six or seven, and he suggested I talk to someone at a local addiction treatment center. I told him I didn't need that because I had been going to AA for years. However, I finally agreed to go talk to someone at the treatment center. I was in a lot of emotional pain and was beginning to realize that I needed help, but I was mortified to think I had become addicted to drugs. I kept asking myself, "How can someone with nearly two decades of sobriety need treatment?" In hindsight, the answer is simple: I was in denial.

I checked into the treatment center and went through a thirty-day program.

I was in detox for the first few days, so I could just stay in my room. I didn't go to meetings or participate in any activities. During this time, my anger was building about the fact that I needed to be there. I had a real chip on my shoulder. But I eventually started participating and accepting the fact that I needed help.

One of the things that helped me was a presentation by a therapist about having a higher power. He explained that you can make your own higher power. It doesn't have to be God. He talked about some of the positive qualities that can be the core of a higher power—such things as being loving, being forgiving, being kind to others, being without jealousy or resentment, and giving to other people.

Then, he explained that when you don't have a higher power, you can become negative. You don't care about other people. You're unkind to others. I realized that this was the type of person I had become. That's when my attitude shifted. Only when I began to listen to the people at the treatment center were they able to help me.

Turning point: It was when I was in the therapist's office and I realized I had a drug problem. I was in so much emotional pain that I knew I needed help.

Advice to others: I usually don't give advice. I just share my story in hopes that it may help others. I do encourage others to go to meetings of AA Narcotics Anonymous if they need help. I also stress that if you want help, you have to give up control. You have to admit that the alcohol or drugs are more powerful than you are, and you can't insist on controlling everything if you want others to help you.

3

Treatment for Addiction

Addiction is a disease—a disease that is treatable. However, research shows that approximately 73 percent of those who are struggling with addiction do not believe they need treatment. Further, only about 17 percent of people seek treatment for addiction, and, of this number, nearly half leave treatment before completing it. Still, treatment can help individuals recover from addiction, making it possible for them to live richer, fuller lives.

There is no "one-size-fits-all" approach to treating addiction. Treatment depends on individual needs and circumstances and the drugs involved. But, for any type of treatment for chemical dependency, the goal is to help individuals make changes in their lives so that they do not need to depend on drugs for coping. Treatment involves learning to make changes in thinking and behaving. And for many, overcoming denial—acceptance that they have a drug problem—is a challenge.

In addition to treatment, follow-up support is important. Research shows that having long-term emotional support after treatment dramatically reduces the risk of relapse.

Types of Treatment

Medical Detoxification

Many individuals are advised to undergo a medical detoxification before beginning a program of treatment or rehabilitation. The purpose of detoxification, or "detox" as it is commonly called, is to help individuals give up addictive substances. Detox is conducted under close medical supervision while patients are going through the withdrawal phase. Withdrawal symptoms may range from mild irritability to seizures and even death. Other common withdrawal symptoms include: anxiety, panic, depression, incoherent thoughts, muscle cramps, vomiting, and nausea.

Most people seeking treatment, nearly three-fourths, undergo detox in a freestanding treatment center; however, detox services can also be offered in hospitals. When patients first enter a detox unit, they are typically given a physical exam, and their medical history is taken. Health professionals are looking for any other underlying physical problems as well as the patient's drug history. It's important for physicians to learn what drugs the patient has been taking and for how long. Then, to ease the symptoms of withdrawal, patients may be given tranquilizers, antihypertensive drugs, or other medications. Some patients may be tapered off the drug they're addicted to.

Detox usually takes several days, perhaps longer, depending on the type of drug to which one is addicted.

Looking for a Treatment Center?

Substance Abuse and Mental Health Services Administration (SAMHSA) offers an online treatment facility locator at www.findtreatment.samhsa.gov. The locator includes more than 12,000 addiction treatment programs, including residential treatment centers, outpatient treatment programs, and hospital inpatient programs for drug addiction and alcoholism.

Some treatment centers have their own medical unit for detoxing. Otherwise, an individual may be referred to an area hospital for detox.

Some detox centers are active in providing individual and group counseling sessions during the time an individual is in the detox unit; other medical units may not offer emotional support. Once the detox is complete, patients are better prepared to enter treatment.

Outpatient Treatment

Outpatient treatment programs, sometimes called partial-day hospital programs or intensive outpatient treatment, can be structured in a number of ways. While undergoing this type of treatment, a patient lives at home and may carry out routine activities during the day—going to work or to school—and then attend treatment programs in the evening. Treatment may involve several hours once or twice a week, or it may require every night of the week.

Similarly, such a program might have patients participating in a treatment program throughout the day, returning home at night. For example, some centers run programs in which patients arrive at the facility Monday through Friday at 8:30 A.M. and stay until 9:00 P.M. The treatment programs vary in length, with some lasting two to three weeks.

The outpatient treatment regimen is usually similar to that of an inpatient program—participating in group therapy sessions, seeing a primary counselor, participating in group counseling sessions, listening to lectures and tapes, and attending twelve-step meetings. The treatment may also involve listening to tapes and lectures on topics such as nutrition, how addiction affects the mind and body, intimacy, sexuality, spirituality, stress, and relapse prevention. Individuals who are very motivated are often considered better candidates for outpatient treatment since they are less likely to drop out of treatment. The outpatient treatment programs may be "medication assisted" or "drug free."

Medication assisted refers to the use of such drugs as Suboxone or methadone, both of which are used for opioid dependence. A drug-free treatment program refers to one that does not use these medications as part of the treatment.

Inpatient Treatment

There are two basic categories of inpatient treatment—hospital based and residential. A hospital-based program is one in which a patient receives a higher level of medical supervision; such treatment would be more appropriate for an individual who has medical conditions or injuries in addition to an addiction disorder. Residential treatment programs are based in nonhospital, freestanding residential centers.

Inpatient programs can be short term or long term. A short-term program is one that lasts fewer than thirty days. Long-term treatment lasts more than thirty days. Both are typically followed by extended outpatient therapy support groups.

Once admitted for inpatient treatment, individuals are usually assigned a primary counselor who will oversee their treatment program. During the inpatient stay, individuals are asked to participate in both individual and group therapy. Treatment programs also may include watching instructional videotapes, listening to lectures, writing assignments, reading materials on recovery, and attending twelve-step meetings. The goal is to teach individuals how to live without drugs and how to avoid situations that could lead to a relapse.

For example, individuals may learn to carefully select the types of company they keep or the places they visit. Does the individual live in an environment where others are using drugs? If so, plans may need to be made to avoid these settings. Does the recovering person avoid reaching out to other people for help? If so, isolation after treatment may trigger a relapse. During treatment, one may identify personality or character issues that may put the individual at risk for relapse.

In short, treatment serves as an education to help the patient answer several key questions: What am I doing to myself emotionally and physically with drugs? What will happen if I continue this habit? How can I stop using drugs? What can I do to stay free of drugs?

These are the kinds of questions Scott, a forty-year-old man from the East Coast, began asking himself as he entered a treatment facility. "I had tried treatment before, but this last time it worked because I really wanted recovery this time. Before, I went into treatment for others—my wife and relatives. But this time I wanted it for myself. I had hit bottom, and I didn't want to live like that anymore. Drugs had robbed me of so much—my business, my family—everything I had worked for. I didn't give treatment a chance before. This last time I did what the professionals told me. I did not try to run my program.

"I'm also learning that I am not just weak. I'm not beating myself up emotionally so much, because I understand now that I have a disease. It's taken me twenty-five years to learn that."

Long-Term or Short-Term Treatment?

Which type of treatment should one consider? It depends on individual circumstances, according to treatment expert William White, senior research assistant with Chestnut Health Systems, which provides chemical-dependency and mental-health services. "Those who benefit from longer treatment are those with more-complex problems, meaning they may have other medical or psychiatric problems that are obstacles to their recovery. Also, those who benefit from longer care are those who have a lack of recovery resources to return to when they go home; they may not have supportive family members or support groups in their communities."

Choosing a Treatment Center

Just as it is important to choose a reputable hospital for any other illness, it is important to choose an addiction treatment center that is operated by qualified personnel. Here are questions patients and families should ask treatment center staff when considering a treatment center for chemical dependency:

- Is there a physician on staff who has been trained in addiction medicine?
- Do the therapists have training and credentials in addiction treatment?
- Is auxiliary treatment available for family members? Recovery is much enhanced if family members understand the dynamics of addiction in a family.
- Does the treatment center teach about relapse? Addiction is prone to relapse, and individuals can learn how to manage it.
- Does the treatment program teach new ways to manage stress? If drugs are no longer used to cope with stress, it's important to develop new coping methods and skills.
- Are twelve-step programs included? These are among the oldest and most successful recovery programs. Are other support programs available, too?
- Does the treatment program help individuals incorporate spirituality into their lives? For some, spirituality may involve religion, but spirituality also refers to all principles that enhance one's sense of purpose and meaning in life.

Importance of Follow-Up Care

Many treatment centers offer follow-up care, often called aftercare. These programs are designed to help prevent relapse in patients who have completed a primary treatment program. Aftercare typically involves individual or group counseling, or both, to provide emotional and spiritual support once or twice a week. The length of aftercare programs varies among treatment centers.

Ongoing emotional support is crucial to recovery, according to treatment expert White. Of today's treatment programs, he says, "We screen patients, admit them, and treat them, but, too often, aftercare is not considered important and the patient relationship is terminated. Severe addiction is a chronic disorder much like diabetes or high blood pressure; you can't treat these diseases in a hospital emergency room—the treatment must be ongoing. Similarly, addiction requires sustained recovery management."

How much ongoing support is needed to sustain recovery? "The research shows that a person's recovery becomes stable after four to five years of ongoing support," explains White. "If you do this, the risk of future relapse drops below 15 percent." The more-progressive treatment programs assign a patient a recovery coach who monitors the patient's recovery through telephone checkups as well as face-to-face interviews.

Forms of Follow-Up Support

Follow-up care may take several forms. It might involve seeing a therapist, or staying in contact with a sponsor from a support group, such as a twelve-step program.

Virtually all treatment programs advocate participation in twelve-step programs, both during aftercare and once aftercare has ended. Two of the best-known groups are Narcotics Anonymous (NA) and Alcoholics Anonymous (AA). The success of such groups is attributed, in part, to the power of the "group dynamic," or the emotional and spiritual support that the members give each other. Consistent participation in these groups helps individuals avoid isolating themselves emotionally. However, the twelve-step groups are not a fit for everyone, so it's important to find the right support group.

Suboxone Treatment

Approved by the Food and Drug Administration (FDA) in 2002, *Suboxone* is a drug treatment for addiction to opioid-based prescription drugs such as painkillers. The generic name of the drug is *buprenorphine* (pronounced: bew-pren-or-feen).

How does Suboxone work? Once ingested, it binds to the same brain cells that opioids bind to, making it impossible for the opioid to enter the brain cells and perpetuate the addiction. To better understand the process, let's use an analogy. Think of the brain as a parking lot. The Suboxone takes up all the parking spaces, leaving none for the opioid.

The Suboxone suppresses withdrawal symptoms once opioids are stopped and greatly reduces or eliminates the craving for drugs. Suboxone does not produce the high or euphoric feeling typically produced by painkillers. If you were to take a painkiller while using Suboxone, you would not feel the usual effects of it.

Starting Suboxone Treatment

In order to start treatment with Suboxone, you must see a physician who has received special training to administer the drug. Several thousand doctors across the nation currently provide the treatment. There is no limit on the number of doctors who can be trained to prescribe the drug; however, each doctor is allowed to treat no more than 100 patients. You can search online for a physician and more information about this drug at www.suboxone.com.

In order to start the drug, you must not be experiencing the effects of opioids. If you have opioids at work in your system and you start taking Suboxone, you can experience what is called a precipitated withdrawal. This is a rapid and intense onset of withdrawal symptoms, caused by the medication. One way of determining whether or not the opioids are still at work is by observing whether you're having withdrawal symptoms. The prescribing physician will make this assessment. The amount of time a person needs to be abstinent from opioids varies among individuals.

Suboxone is taken sublingually, meaning it sits under your tongue. The first dose is given in the doctor's office. Then, patients are typically given a thirty-day prescription and the drug is taken once daily. Beginning doses are usually higher and then are reduced to a maintenance level during the course of treatment. Follow-up visits with the doctor are required. The goal is to eventually be tapered off the drug completely.

How long do you take this drug? There is no single answer to this question. The length of time varies among patients. Many people who do well with the program stay on Suboxone for six to eighteen months before being slowly tapered off the drug; some stay on it much longer.

Individuals who start taking Suboxone are also encouraged to seek counseling. Research shows that those who receive therapy and/or attend support groups have a better outcome than those who only take the drug.

My Experience with Suboxone
Rose, 31

I have been taking Suboxone for two years. It has allowed me to get my life back to normal. I was addicted to painkillers for about a year and a half. I first took Vicodin for pain after having a root canal done. I loved the way the drug made me feel. I wanted to take more, and didn't realize they were highly addictive. I worked in a medical clinic, where I began to steal drugs and phone in my own prescriptions to a pharmacy. Eventually, I was discovered and fired from my job.

When I tried to stop the drug, I would have terrible withdrawals—anxiety, muscle twitches, nausea, vomiting, and diarrhea. It was like the flu, only ten times worse. I did enter an intensive outpatient treatment program, but was still struggling with the addiction. Then, my boyfriend's mother sent me an article on Suboxone from a newspaper.

I found a doctor who could prescribe the drug. He did an extensive interview with me and decided I would be a good candidate for Suboxone. I had a rough first week; I'm not sure why, but I had some feelings of withdrawal. But then, in the second week, I started to feel normal for the first time in years. I had no withdrawal symptoms. I wasn't craving drugs and trying to come up with schemes to get drugs. I started sleeping better. It was pretty remarkable. I have been able to go to work and make good choices in my life.

Methadone Treatment

In the past, you may have heard more about methadone as a treatment for heroin addiction; however, in the past few years, more people have begun methadone treatment for addiction to prescription opioids such as OxyContin, Dilaudid, and Vicodin. In fact, in some states, nearly half the people in methadone programs are being treated for addiction to prescription narcotics. In the United States, there are 1,150 methadone clinics in forty-seven states.

Methadone is a synthetic agent that works by "occupying" the brain receptor sites affected by opiates. It blocks the euphoric and sedating effects of opiates and relieves the cravings for them. In stable doses, methadone does not cause intoxication. It comes in the form of solid tablets, premixed liquid, or dispersible tablets that must be dissolved in a glass of water.

Methadone Clinics

To receive methadone treatment for addiction, you must go to a methadone clinic and participate in a highly structured program. Methadone clinics are under tight federal and state control, and initially, methadone doses are given only at the clinics. Those just starting a program must go to the clinic daily, six days a week, for the first three months. Once participants have demonstrated stability in treatment, they may begin going to the clinic five days a week and getting one take-home dose. Over the next few months, if the patient shows treatment stability, fewer visits to the clinic are required and more take-home doses are given.

The well-run methadone programs also include appropriate screening and physical examinations, counseling, regular medical reviews, treatment planning, and follow-up. To be eligible for such a program, you must be at least eighteen years old and have been addicted to opiates for one year or more.

Why do some individuals seek methadone treatment? "Methadone is a medication that pharmacologically helps a certain group of people who haven't succeeded in other programs," according to Mark Parrino, President of the American Association for the Treatment of Opioid Dependence, Inc. "Methadone seems to help those who have a high degree of addiction and who have been addicted to opiates for a long period of time."

Some people can eventually be tapered off methadone; others will need to take it for years, possibly for life. The length of the treatment depends on the individual. A person who has been addicted to narcotics for a year will have needs that differ from those who have been addicted for fifteen years.

Urgent Need for Patient Education

It is crucial that anyone taking methadone understands how to use the drug appropriately. In 2005, there were nearly 4,500 methadone-related deaths. That is an increase of 500 percent from 1999. "When used as prescribed, it is a safe and effective medication, but it can cause death when misused," says Parrino. "The research shows that many of the deaths involving methadone occurred in patients who had prescriptions of methadone for pain." In recent years, more doctors have begun prescribing methadone for pain. In 2006, doctors wrote 4 million prescriptions for methadone; in 1998, they wrote only half a million prescriptions.

Patients need to understand clearly how to use the drug safely, and doctors need to prescribe it properly and safely. It can be a complicated drug to prescribe. The painkilling properties of the drug may fade in a few hours, but the drug can stay in the bloodstream for days. A patient may hope to get more pain relief, so he or she takes an additional dose, but the drug can build up in the bloodstream to a lethal level, and the patient stops breathing.

Methadone patients need to also understand the dangers of the so-called "poisonous cocktail," in which methadone is mixed with other narcotics or alcohol. The combination of drugs being taken together can cause respiratory depression and death.

My Experience with Methadone
Paul, 45

I got hooked on painkillers in the late 1990s. I had undergone a fairly minor surgical procedure and was prescribed pain pills. I took them as directed and started to really like the way they made me feel. So eventually, I started going to multiple doctors to get pills. It was easy to get drugs. I could even tell some doctors what drugs I wanted. If a doctor cut me off, I would move on to other doctors. I was taking drugs such as Percocet, Vicodin, and OxyContin.

When I ran out of pills and went into withdrawal, I would get terribly sick. At the time, I didn't realize it was withdrawal. I even went to emergency rooms because I felt so sick—I would be vomiting and have headaches. I had been hooked on the painkillers for about three years before I started to realize I had a drug problem.

I did some research on methadone treatment for opioid dependence and thought I would try it. I tried several times to get into a treatment program but getting in wasn't easy. There were waiting lists to get into the programs in my area. Eventually, I got in and started treatment. I was on methadone for five years.

The drug helped me immediately. I was no longer getting sick from withdrawal. I wasn't constantly worrying about lying to doctors so I could get more pain pills. I was able to go to work and get back to a normal life.

In the beginning, I had to go to the methadone clinic every morning to get my dose for the day; it was in liquid form. It was only after a few months of being a compliant patient that I was given take-home dosages. These treatment programs are very tightly controlled. For example, if I was given six take-home dosages, the program office could call me at any time and ask me to bring my methadone dosages and come in for a random check. They wanted to make sure I had not used more than one dose a day.

While I was on methadone treatment, I also started going to counseling and learning a lot about addiction, which was very helpful. I learned that addiction is a disease and not a character defect. I think education is the key for anyone trying to recover from an addiction. However, it's sort of a catch-22 in that it is hard to focus on education if you're still addicted; it helps to have your disease stable so that you're able and ready to receive education.

Methadone helped me get my life back. However, after five years of being on it, I switched to the drug Suboxone. I changed drugs because I had become stable in my recovery, and Suboxone could be prescribed by a doctor without the structure of the program that is part of methadone treatment.

Still, I support methadone as an important form of treatment for opioid dependence. I now serve as a regional director for a methadone advocacy organization, and I believe in the drug and how it can help people...if it's in the right hands. However, I have a concern about people getting take-home prescriptions for pain. If misused or taken by another member of a family, such as a teenager, the drug can have lethal consequences.

Rapid-Detox Treatment

Rapid-detox centers began appearing in the United States in the mid-1990s. As the name implies, the detoxification is completed rapidly, ridding the patient of cravings and withdrawal symptoms within a matter of hours rather than over a period of days in a conventional treatment center. Done while the patient is under general anesthesia, rapid-detox treatment is only for opiate addiction.

The Rapid-Detox Procedure

One treatment program offering rapid detox is located at Texas Tech University Health Sciences Center. Patients are chosen only after careful screening and must demonstrate a desire to get off the opiates. The treatment is carried out in the intensive care unit, where body and brain wave activity can be monitored.

"Before we put patients to sleep we give them a drug that neutralizes the body's ability to become hyper or aroused," explains Dr. Alan Kaye, who heads the rapid-detox program. "Once we're ready to begin, the patient is given a general anesthetic. Then, we give the patient a massive amount of an opiate *antagonist*, or a drug that blocks the opiate." Then, over a six-hour period, while the patient is asleep, he or she goes through withdrawal. "Essentially, all the opiates are wiped off the brain's receptor sites. It's done humanely because the patient is not awake," states Kaye.

When the individual awakens, he or she is given another opiate blocker, which is taken orally for six months. This drug is intended to decrease cravings and block an opiate from having any effect if the individual should relapse.

Many programs include ongoing counseling, to help avoid relapse, as part of the treatment. The cost of a rapid-detox procedure may range from $5,000 to upwards of $15,000.

Is Rapid Detox Safe?

Although thousands of successful rapid-detox procedures have been performed in the United States, there have also been some deaths. The safety of the treatment is still the subject of controversy. Some medical and addiction specialists say there is risk of death anytime general anesthesia is used. The American Society of Addiction Medicine (ASAM) does not endorse the treatment, stating that additional research should be completed to confirm both the procedure's efficacy and safety. According to ASAM, most of the procedure's risk is related to the experience and expertise of the anesthesiologist and other medical personnel carrying out the procedure.

Relapse Prevention

Recovery does not end once you've come off a drug. In fact, this just marks the beginning of recovery, and it's important to realize that relapse can be common with addiction. Relapse refers to an individual's return to drug use after a period of abstinence. One of the nation's experts on relapse prevention, Terence Gorski, a nationally recognized recovery and relapse prevention specialist and author of *Staying Sober* (www.tgorski.com), says people who are coming off drugs are often unaware of the sobriety-based symptoms. Gorksi describes these symptoms as being "post acute withdrawal syndrome," or PAWS, and they include: inability to think clearly, memory problems, emotional overreactions or numbness, sleep disturbances, physical coordination problems, and sensitivity to stress.

Gorski explains it's important to be aware of these symptoms and understand that they are often part of early recovery. Understanding PAWS can help avoid relapse.

If you or someone in your life has a relapse, don't give up. Addiction is a chronic disease, and many recovering individuals experience relapses before sustaining sobriety. A "slip" may be discouraging, but it should never be considered the end of recovery.

"There is no such thing as a hopeless addict. There are only those who haven't found out about relapse prevention techniques," says Gorski. "Learning how to be sober is a skill-training experience. You have to learn to depend on something besides alcohol or drugs to deal with your thoughts, feelings, relationships, and behaviors. Basically, relapse prevention therapy is based upon the premise that there are observable warning signs that occur before a person returns to alcohol or drug use."

According to Gorski, most relapses can be attributed to the "triggers" outlined below:

- Stress or change occurs in a person's life.
- The stressor triggers a change in thinking. The individual begins using old, addictive thinking strategies, which then trigger a change in feeling.
- The individual begins to experience painful, distressful, unmanageable feelings.
- These feelings produce a change in behavior. The person begins using self-defeating or compulsive behaviors to cope with the feelings.
- The individual starts associating with people, places, and things that tolerate his or her self-destructive behavior.

With the Gorski PAWS model in mind, what should you do to prevent relapse? To manage post-withdrawal symptoms, Gorksi recommends having a solid support system—people whom you can vent to; people who will help protect you from stress; people who encourage you to exercise, get plenty of rest, and eat nutritious meals.

What else can you do to avoid relapse? First, identify your own unique pattern of relapse warning signs. Every recovering person has relapse warning signs. They are like fingerprints—everybody has them, but each person's are different. Write down your list of relapse warning signs and describe how they move you from stable recovery back toward alcohol or drug use. Seek feedback from outside

Lifesaving Alert!

One of the dangers of relapse is having the mistaken belief that, should you return to taking drugs, you can consume the same amount of opioids as you did at the peak of your addiction, when your tolerance was high. However, within weeks of being off an addictive drug, your tolerance is reduced significantly. If you were to take the same high doses as before, you risk a potentially fatal overdose. Many shocked and devastated family members have been heard to say, "He hadn't used drugs for several months. He was doing so well, but then he was found dead from an overdose."

sources, because the recovering person is locked in a delusional system and can't always see what's really going on in life.

"One of the most important things I've learned about recovery is that if you've been dependent on drugs or alcohol, you cannot safely use these substances," Gorski explains. "The goal needs to be to learn how to live a drug-free life. To do this, you have to learn how to think clearly, logically, and rationally in a sober state. You need to learn how to recognize, label, and communicate your feelings and emotions in a sober state. And you have to learn how to self-regulate your behavior as a sober person. You must readjust from an addiction-centered social life to a sobriety-centered social life."

According to Gorski, addiction has three facets—biological, psychological, and social dependence. People can become dependent on any one of these levels or all three simultaneously. Biological dependence refers to a tissue dependency on a drug, which then creates tolerance and withdrawal. With psychological dependence, a person has come to rely on drugs or alcohol in order to manage their thinking, feeling, and behaviors. Without these substances, they can't think clearly or deal with feelings. They can't self-regulate their behaviors. Social dependence indicates that a person has come to rely on alcohol or drugs to act as a social lubricant or social facilitator; without these, they cannot maintain satisfactory relationships with others.

Does Insurance Pay for Drug Rehab?

Some insurance companies do pay for addiction treatment or portions of it; however, over the past decade, insurance companies have become more restrictive in paying for both inpatient and outpatient treatment.

Treatment Is Cost Effective

Treating substance abuse not only saves lives, but also saves dollars for society. It is estimated that untreated addiction in the United States costs about $300 billion a year, or an average of $1,000 per person annually. These costs include such things as medical treatment for injuries, traffic accidents, crime, and days lost in the workplace. Yet, if the nation were paying for treatment for every addicted person in the country, the average cost per person would be $45 per year.

A study by the National Institute on Drug Abuse found that each dollar spent on addiction treatment saves $4 to $7 in reduced medical and social costs, and returns $3 in increased worker productivity. The study concluded that each dollar invested in treatment returns $7 to $10 to society.

4

Insights on Recovery from Addiction Medicine Physicians

All too often, individuals in recovery say they didn't seek treatment early enough or they went to health professionals who didn't understand or diagnose their addiction. Consequently, proper treatment was delayed. Because addiction is an illness that requires first diagnosis and then treatment, it is important that we avail ourselves of those health professionals who understand chemical dependency and how it is treated.

In this chapter, you'll hear from experts on addiction, including addictionologists from the American Society of Addiction Medicine (ASAM), who have treated thousands of individuals for chemical dependency. ASAM is an international association of 3,000 physicians dedicated to improving the treatment of alcoholism and other addictions.

Addiction Is an Illness

Sidney Schnoll, M.D.
Addictionologist

Our culture today too often looks upon addicts as we did epileptics 400 years ago—we burned them at the stake because we thought they were possessed. Today, we know that people with drug addiction have a disease that requires specific treatment. People who are addicted are suffering from an illness, just as one suffers from diabetes or any other illness. Yet, many addicts are viewed as having something morally wrong with them—as if it's something they bring upon themselves.

I became interested in substance abuse and addiction more than thirty years ago when I was a resident at Philadelphia General Hospital. I saw a lot of young people coming in with problems from LSD use. No one quite knew how to take care of them.

There is no one treatment for most diseases. And so, there is no one specific treatment for addiction. We're talking about roads to recovery, rather than one road to recovery. There is not one shoe that fits all. I think one of the biggest mistakes made in the field of addiction is that people make the assumption that there's one way to recover and if you don't do it that way, there's something wrong with you. For example, not every diabetic needs insulin. And those who get it take different doses. And diabetics have different courses of progression in their disease. The same is true for addiction. It is a chronic disease just like diabetes. We can treat it, but we cannot cure it. We can control some of the symptoms. We can make some people's lives very comfortable; other people do not do as well.

Anyone who needs help with addiction should seek out the assistance of someone trained in the diagnosis and assessment of the problems of addiction. Addiction is not something that most physicians are adequately prepared to treat.

Building on Hope

LeClair Bissell, M.D.
Addictionologist

I'm a recovering alcoholic, so I became interested in recovery issues during my own recovery. Some years later, I went to medical school and went on to practice addiction medicine full time. My writing and research has dealt almost exclusively with substance abuse and chemical dependency.

If someone who's battling addiction feels hopeless, I would offer them the experience of other people who have recovered, along with the understanding of what the patient is feeling emotionally at the moment. Empathy without sentimentality. Also, if they're feeling really hopeless, I would make a note to myself to see if there have been suicide attempts, and if so, how many. I'd also want to evaluate for depression. If one has come to treatment on his own, he must have a pinch of hope that things might get better; otherwise, he wouldn't be there.

When it comes to treating prescription drug addiction, there are some attitudinal differences when comparing it to alcoholism. For example, a good many individuals might think it's naughty to drink, but that it's okay to have certain sedative-hypnotic pills if the doctor has prescribed them. The truth is, these drugs are in the same "family" as alcohol. But pills aren't seen as being as bad as alcohol.

And all too often, these addicts are hard to spot for doctors who haven't had the training. If the patient comes in with a clean white shirt and clean fingernails—not the stereotype of the drug addict—many doctors will not realize the patient is an addict. The diagnosis of addiction is often made by caste and class and is made late rather than early.

If you are an addict or alcoholic in recovery, it's very important to tell your doctor so that you aren't given addictive drugs or cough syrups with alcohol. Doctors need to take a patient's history before prescribing drugs. We need to use these drugs of addiction as little and for as short a time as possible.

Over the years, I saw many patients who were doing quite well in recovery from alcoholism, but went to a physician and were given sedatives or tranquilizers. Then their mood swings began, and ultimately, they began to drink again. When someone in a case like this takes the sedatives and then a couple of drinks, they become very relaxed. But in a matter of a few hours, they're going to be more tense than when they started. That's when they're in rebound, the return of original symptoms which is part of withdrawal. They're having these intense emotional ups and downs. If you're an alcoholic, you already have a body that knows perfectly well what you can do when those up periods feel too uncomfortable—you use more chemicals.

I'm not saying anything whatsoever about the minor use of tranquilizers by people who are not addicts. There's quite a body of information that says these drugs are pretty safe for occasional use. But for those who have already had problems with alcohol or other drugs, it's a bad idea to start taking other mood-changing drugs.

I always give this word of warning about drugs of addiction: Whenever you take a drug and it really changes the way you feel, makes you feel really good—be careful. It may be something you should not have.

Let me stress that there are untold thousands who can use drugs wisely. But as a doctor in addiction medicine, I've seen only the casualties over the years. I never saw the patients who took only a few pills and used them wisely. I saw people who got into bad trouble and then came to me for help. I would say to those recovering from prescription drug addiction: Be patient. It may be a while before you feel a lot better. I saw this especially with benzodiazepines. For example, someone could be clean for two months and still not feel well. It's easy to get discouraged and go back to the pills. They need to hang on—it won't always be as bad.

Finally, I would like to share some thoughts with families. As part of my work, I also saw many family members who suffered deeply because of a loved one's addiction. When family and friends are trying to cope with an addict, it's important for them to understand several things. One, the relative or friend has to realize that they did not cause the problem and they cannot, by themselves, resolve it. Even if the addict is blaming them, they must realize they're not responsible.

Equally important, the relative has got to stop making it easy for the addict to stay sick. The parent who constantly pays the fine or bails his kid out of jail is enabling. The addict does not have to face the consequences of his or her own behavior.

Another important thing for the family to know is what a doctor recommends for the patient, if treatment is underway. For example, the patient might visit a doctor and then go home and tell the family the doctor said it was okay to take a drink or a few drugs once in a while. It helps if the family knows that the physician has recommended *total* abstinence from alcohol and all other mood-changing drugs of addiction.

Be Cautious with Benzodiazepines

Ronald Gershman, M.D.
Addictionologist

I was a psychiatrist in private practice for twenty years. Most of that time, I worked in the treatment of chemical dependency. I treated about 10,000 patients for alcohol and drug problems and detoxed approximately 1,500 patients for benzodiazepines, a strong focus of mine.

When it comes to treating patients, I see two patterns. First, there is essentially the drug addict who supports an addiction through the use of prescription pills. These patients see themselves as different from other addicts; they often think their prescribed medication is justified even though they may be manipulating and deceptive in acquiring excessive amounts of drugs. Second, I see the individuals we call the "unwitting" or "iatrogenic" addicts. These patients were put on medication (especially benzodiazepines) for legitimate reasons, but for an extended period of time, and they became addicted.

How do such addictions occur? Benzodiazepines aside for a moment, let's look at opiates, which are commonly used to treat pain. When people take an opiate medication, the drug relieves physical pain and it also relieves emotional pain. The problem of abuse comes in using the drug to relieve emotional pain.

For most patients, if they're using the drug strictly to relieve physical pain, when the physical pain is gone, they can give up the drug. But if they're depressed or anxious or life is miserable for them, then the drug use can become a problem after the physical pain is eliminated. The emotional pain is still there and they still want to treat that pain. From what I've seen, this is a pretty clear pattern, but it's not easy to tell which patients might end up seeking the drug for emotional pain once they've healed physically.

The treatment for addiction differs dramatically, depending on the nature of the drug you're treating. For example, treatment for a benzodiazepine addiction is very different from treatment for an opiate such as Vicodin or codeine.

Managing the withdrawal and keeping the patient from relapsing is the real crux of the problem. The detox for opiates is about seven to ten days and can usually be done on an outpatient basis. I used about eight different medications to help patients get through detox. Among the medications we used was an opiate blocker, which prevented an opiate from "working" if the patient relapsed. We also used antidepressants because the depressions are quite severe and are a major cause of relapse. Then, with therapy, we helped the patient learn to live and manage a sober life, which is really the heart and soul of the work that needs to be done. Detox is usually quite successful if the patient is highly motivated.

But detox for benzodiazepines is more difficult. It takes longer, ranging perhaps from six to eighteen months. In this recovery, the ongoing, relentless withdrawals can be incapacitating. The "fallout" from addiction to these drugs can lead to the breakup of marriages, the loss of businesses, and hospitalizations. Unfortunately, suicide is probably the single most serious side effect.

All too often, doctors do not recognize this withdrawal pattern. The patient has been on the drugs for a year or so and then the doctor says, "I don't think you need these anymore," and takes them off. In a few days, when the patient breaks down, the doctor and patient assume the "old psychiatric problem" is returning. The patient is hospitalized and put on drugs. This cycle can prevent getting to the root of the dependency problem.

If benzodiazepines are used inappropriately and the patient becomes addicted, the patient builds tolerance and the drugs stop working. In fact, over a long period of time, their usage can worsen the condition they were being used to treat. What happens is, the level of the drug in the blood drops between doses, which quickly brings on withdrawal symptoms. So the drug is losing its effectiveness, while the withdrawal is making symptoms three or four times worse than they were before.

I believe benzodiazepines are appropriate for short-term management of acute anxiety or panic attacks. Short-term use generally means two to six weeks, the absolute maximum I would recommend.

Using Benzodiazepines Responsibly

David Mee-Lee, M.D.
Addictionologist

There is disagreement in the medical community about the use of benzodiazepines. Although some say benzodiazepines are overused, others would say the opposite, that they're being underutilized out of doctors' concerns that patients will become addicted.

Opinions vary, even by country. Britain has been very strict in limiting use of benzodiazepines to shorter-term use. In the United States, the fear of abuse has been overblown and patients are being robbed of adequate use because of fear of addiction.

My view is that these drugs are like alcohol, in that not everyone is going to use them inappropriately. I think long-term use can be acceptable as long as the risks and benefits are weighed cautiously and careful assessment of the patient is done to make sure those at high risk for addiction are screened out.

Even if a patient is not at high risk for addiction, the physician should always periodically reassess the use of any medication to see if the patient still needs it. I don't believe drugs should be prescribed blindly just because the patient is not becoming addicted. There are other ways to cope.

Of course, anyone taking even therapeutic doses of a benzodiazepine for a period of time will become tolerant of the drug and will have to be gradually withdrawn from it. To quit abruptly would cause withdrawal. But not everyone would have to be detoxed on an inpatient basis.

The people who often get in trouble are those who have escalated their use of the drug; they take high dosages and are often in a poor recovery environment. They may also lack emotional support and have poor impulse control in terms of relapse. Most people will do better if they have motivation to come off the drug and have resources, both personal and environmental, to help them deal with impulsive use.

We need to understand a couple of basics about addiction. One, addiction affects not only the person using, but those around them—family and friends. There are very few families who aren't affected by addiction in some way. Also, the one who has the problem needs to acknowledge that there is a problem. Family members and others can be helpful by confronting and not rescuing the person.

The patients who obtain pharmaceuticals through legal means, but yet escalate dosages and abuse the drugs, often have trouble admitting their problem. They tend to say they were just doing what their doctors told them. They don't see themselves as addicts. We try to help these patients see that their drug use has been negatively affecting their lives. Some of these patients come to treatment once their doctor has judged they've become addicted and has stopped prescribing. The patients are sometimes left not knowing what to do if they're not guided into treatment.

What goes into successful recovery? Anyone *can* succeed. But the degree of difficulty in recovering depends on how much damage has already been done. Has the patient lost jobs, family, and physical health? The more one has lost, the harder recovery might be.

Recovery from addiction is similar to recovering from other chronic illnesses. You have to keep monitoring it to make sure you're taking care of yourself. It means continuing in some kind of recovery program. That doesn't mean going to support groups daily for the rest of your life, but rather continuing to be vigilant about relapse and using support groups or other methods to stay aware.

Some people can recover with little help—not everyone goes through treatment. They come to the awareness that they have a problem and decide to do something about it. However, many others need help.

And in the scenario in which the addict won't go into recovery, his or her family can still recover. They can learn to stop playing into the addict's agenda and learn to stop passing the problem on down through generation after generation.

In short, people with chemical dependencies must first admit that they have an illness; second, realize they're at risk for relapse; and third, recognize that they need ways to cope with stress or problems if they're heading toward relapse. Addiction is a chronic illness, not a moral problem. It needs treatment, not judgment.

Stages of Chemical Dependence

Stage	Description
Abstinence	Person has not begun to use the drug, but attitudes are developing
Nonproblem use	No negative consequences of use
High-risk use	Use is frequent, heavy, or usage patterns are dangerous
Problem use (or abuse)	First negative consequences arise from usage patterns
Chemical dependence: Early stage	Reversible, less-serious negative consequences of threats do not motivate corrective adjustment of usage patterns
Chemical dependence: Middle stage	Irreversible negative consequences of use do not motivate significant corrective adjustment of usage patterns
Chemical dependence: Late stage	Multiple, serious, irreversible negative consequences have failed to motivate corrective adjustment of usage patterns

From "Finding Substance Abusers" by M.P. et al., 1984. *Family Medicine Curriculum Guide to Substance Abuse* (Society for Teachers of Family Medicine, Kansas City, Missouri). Reprinted by permission.

Addiction and Denial

Patrick Dalton
Certified Addiction Counselor

The individuals we see are outpatients. Many are addicted to prescription drugs. We insist that they divulge all information about the drugs they are taking in order for us to treat them effectively. Often, they're getting drugs from doctors who aren't aware of addiction issues. The doctor might be trying to eliminate a patient's pain but not understand potential addiction problems. If the patient is prone to addiction, this can be like pouring gasoline on a fire.

Those dependent on prescription drugs have a mind-set different from that of alcoholics. Most of the people I've treated are very resistant to letting go of their drugs. They can partially justify it because they've gotten their drugs legitimately, from a doctor. They don't have the stigma of being a user of street drugs. This causes a high degree of relapse. In addition to this denial, those who are prescription-drug dependent have a real fear of not being able to cope without their drugs. They are very "med-seeking," always wanting a pill to fix them.

Some people don't realize they are prone to addiction, and they get hooked on a legal drug. They may not realize it until they start having negative consequences in their lives. When you use a chemical of any kind, once it has brought negative consequences to your life, you're crossing the line into addiction. Anyone who is aware of his or her addictive tendencies should always tell a treating physician.

Realizing Risk for Addiction

Sheila Blume, M.D.
Addictionologist

Not everyone who takes painkillers or sedatives gets addicted, but anyone who does take them should be warned of their addictive potential. In my experience, those who become addicted to these drugs fall into several categories.

The most common is the person who is an alcoholic but doesn't know it—the alcoholism hasn't been diagnosed, and the person is being seen for associated symptoms such as insomnia, tension, and difficulty concentrating. Then, an addictive drug is prescribed and the patient becomes addicted.

Equally unfortunate is the patient who has recovered from alcoholism but does not understand the potential of other drugs and becomes addicted to them. These people may have recovered from earlier addictions on their own, without treatment or self-help groups. Many, many people do this. However, if they haven't been in a treatment program, they may not have been educated about other mood-altering drugs. Having this knowledge could have saved many self-recovering people from additional trouble.

I recall the case of one man, a recovering alcoholic, who had dislocated his shoulder. Because he had stopped using alcohol on his own, he really didn't see himself as an alcoholic. So, when he was given Tylenol with Codeine for pain, he got hooked on it and, in the end, it almost killed him.

All recovering addicts need to tell any doctor, including dentists, that they should not be given habit-forming drugs. If a doctor tells a recovering patient that the drugs won't cause dependency problems, but the patient still isn't sure, he or she should check with the pharmacist about any such dangers with the drug.

Another category of people who are susceptible to dependence are those in a lot of emotional distress or agitation. Once prescribed a sedative or tranquilizer, they can become dependent. For people who have not been drug dependent before, the first symptom of dependence is that the drug becomes very precious to them. They always make sure they have it with them at all times. They have the prescription refilled as soon as possible so they won't run out. The drug helps them, and they think it is the most wonderful thing in the world.

Then, when they hit a point where something bothers them emotionally, they take more of the drug and that feels good. They begin to increase the dose. At this point, they may get wary and decide not to tell their doctor about how they're using the drug. They fear their doctor won't approve and will stop prescribing. They begin to justify their use of the drug through denial or rationalization. They might start to manipulate the doctor, saying they lost a prescription or they're going on a trip and need extra pills. This works for only a short time, so then they'll have to switch to another doctor. They may have five or six doctors they can reliably go to.

They know exactly what drug they want when they schedule an appointment.

There is a point when abuse becomes addiction. Abuse refers to dangerous use, like taking a drug and driving when you should not be driving under the influence of the drug. Often, people can stop at abuse, but if they don't, they move on to dependence.

My message of hope is that prescription drug addiction is a treatable disease. Sometimes it's harder to do an intervention with prescription drugs than with alcohol or illegal drugs. Patients often believe they really don't need treatment. But treatment can help them return to a productive life. Recovery is very possible.

Addicts Are Not Having Fun

Howard Heit, M.D.
Addictionologist/Pain Specialist

When a person who needs treatment is reluctant to get help, I ask, "Are you having a good time?" The patient is usually taken aback by that because even though the public perceives that addicts are having a good time, the addict knows deep down that he or she is *not* having a good time. I remind them that they're not.

Why aren't they? First, they wake up each day worrying about their supply of pills, whether they're going to be able to "work" doctors for more drugs, or get drugs illicitly, which is very expensive. Second, they have a poor quality of life, given their drug-seeking behavior. So, if they're not having a good time, and their habit is expensive, degrading, and scary, I ask, "Why not try a program of recovery?" Most people will eventually agree.

I explain the kinds of changes that they have to make to stay in recovery. And, very early when they're having some difficulties making changes, I give them this homework assignment.

I ask them, "How long does it take you to drive home?"

"Half an hour," they may say.

"I want you to take an hour, take a long way home. And on your way home, I want you to count the number of dinosaurs that you see."

This causes them to stop and ponder my suggestion. "I'm not going to see any dinosaurs."

"Exactly," I respond. "The dinosaurs didn't adapt. They didn't survive. And now you have to make these adaptations or changes in your life if you want to stay on Earth. I will help you, but it takes work."

If they choose to work with me, I first take a very thorough medical history. The overwhelming majority of times, these are good people, solid people, intelligent. But, in their history, I might find such things as a sleep disorder, depression, or a psychiatric problem that has gone undiagnosed and untreated. These underlying causes are partly to blame for them using the drugs excessively and becoming addicted. I validate what has happened to them and again explain why their body has become used to or physically dependent on these medicines.

Consider the benzodiazepine Xanax, for example. I explain to a patient that I can safely wean him or her off Xanax by switching to a long-acting benzodiazepine. I point out that a short-acting benzodiazepine like Xanax has what we call an "off-and-on switch." That is, the level of Xanax in the blood fluctuates off and on, up and down, giving one the positive reinforcement, the craving, and the alteration of the biological and physiological system. These cravings kick in like clockwork with short-acting benzos, and the majority of the drugs of abuse are short acting.

I explain that I'm going to switch them to another drug in the same class that will go to the same receptor site on the brain, but it's a long-acting medication. Therefore, instead of falling off and on the receptor site, it will stay there for a twenty-four-hour period. Then what I do is slowly reduce the dose so that the brain gets used to slow reduction of the drug, and we wean them off the medication. We never want to stop the benzo abruptly, since doing so can cause seizures.

I may further explain that I have also noted in their medical history a sleep disorder or other emotional problem. "It sounds like you have anxiety or are depressed. While we're working on this, let me place you on another medication—one that is nonaddictive—to help you with the sleep problem."

Here, I also stress the importance of changing behaviors. In the past, this patient conditioned himself or herself to reach for a pill when life becomes stressful. I introduce them to what I call a "Thoughts, Feelings, Actions, and Alternatives Diary." I ask them to record what happens when they feel the need to take a pill. They may write, "I want to take a Xanax. Why do I want to take a Xanax? I'm sad. My action is to take a Xanax. Wait a minute. What is my alternative? Maybe I will go and speak to my significant other and resolve this difficulty that we're having."

As another part of the treatment, I may also bring in a trained therapist to work on identifying and handling the "trigger points"—those stressors that make them want to use the drug. And so the recovery process is underway.

In short, the process works like this: You have the powerful primitive part of the brain that likes the feelings drugs bring; I call this part the "dark angel." And you have the "white angel," the intellectual part of the brain that handles thoughts, feelings, and actions. The task is to bring in the white angel to handle the dysfunctional trigger points that lead to destructive behaviors.

Warning Signs of Addiction

David Gastfriend, M.D.
Addictionologist

I would say about 15 percent of our practice involves prescription drug dependence. We see a range of patients. At one end of the range are patients who have been prescribed a drug from the Valium family, like Xanax, for treatment of panic disorder. Initially they got relief from the drug, but then needed increased doses to achieve their state of comfort. Then they have difficulty coming off the medication, even though they want to discontinue it. This is a case of physiological dependence, not addiction, and it's very common with these medications even when they are used correctly and safely. Treatment is a matter of tapering the doses, educating the patient about what to expect, and teaching the patient to use behavioral techniques to cope with modest withdrawal symptoms. This is the most common problem we see.

At the other end of the range are those who are fully dependent on either alcohol, cocaine, or narcotics and are compulsively seeking to get high. They will use prescription drugs in combination with illegal drugs. Or, when they can't get heroin, they'll substitute with prescription opiates or benzodiazepines. They are truly addicted, manipulative, and compelled by their disease to beat the system. Often they feign illness to multiple doctors. These patients make up a smaller element of the overall problem, but it's a very costly problem in terms of death, emergency room visits, thefts, auto accidents, firearm accidents, and drug trading.

The mid-range of patients that I see are those who have been prescribed medications and who have psychological problems, although these problems initially may not have been apparent. Such problems include dependency on others, impulsiveness under stress, and paranoia. For these patients, certain drugs can create physiological and psychological dependence. This begins the cycle of addiction—compulsive use—resulting in an urge to use the substance at high personal costs.

We know there are individuals who are highly vulnerable to becoming alcoholic for genetic reasons, but we don't have reliable research on genetic vulnerability to addiction to anxiety medications and prescription narcotics. However, there are studies that infer that the same genetic vulnerability exists. Many drugs have the same physiological effects as alcohol.

Patients in this category are often referred to us addiction specialists once their doctors realize they're being manipulated into prescribing excessive doses. The doctor may not want to cut off the patient completely from the drug and will call for a consultation with an addiction specialist.

There are warning signs that indicate prescription drug use is becoming problematic. Addiction problems could be arising when:

- You start to feel that the drug, at the same dose, isn't working as well as it used to.
- You feel the drug wearing off before it's time to take the next dose.
- You experience more than symptom relief as the drug takes effect; there is some degree of excitement or high. This indicates the dose may be excessive or that the medication may work too rapidly for safe, long-term use.
- You feel subdued or lethargic within a few hours of taking the medication. This may be an another indication that the dose is excessive.
- You're irritable and have problems sleeping. Here, the medication may be too short acting and may produce mild withdrawal over the course of the sleep cycle.
- You feel that you can perform certain tasks or engage in certain activities (like driving through traffic or socializing at a party) only with the benefit of the medication. This feeling increases with time.

If you note any of these warning signs, you should speak to your physician. Consider a consultation with an addiction specialist. Also, review your past history and your family history for substance use. Did your parents, grandparents, or siblings have problems with medications or substances like alcohol?

If a patient has run into problems with a drug, we expect them to take some responsibility for their behavior and ask for help. Many are afraid to ask questions for fear they'll be cut off from the drug and they'll suffer. But in order to reasonably and ethically prescribe some of these medications, the physician counts on the patient to be a partner in fostering good health.

Support Groups Help Avoid Isolation

Jeff Baldwin, Pharm.D.
Associate Professor of Pharmacy

It's important to recognize that there's not a specific level of drug or alcohol use that determines when you're addicted. For example, I've seen a woman who was alcoholic on one beer a day, and I've seen a man who was alcoholic on a case of beer a day. The better definition of addiction is "continuing to use a substance once it brings negative consequences to your life."

Once we do have an addiction, I believe one of the most important things for recovering is faithfully going to meetings, twelve-step or support groups. And recovering people who first go to twelve-step groups also should understand that they may need to be on some medications during their recovery. Although they mean well, some people attending those meetings may say that if you're taking any drug that has mood-altering properties, you are not "clean." I do not agree with these individuals. In fact, some 40 percent of alcoholics and addicts have a dual diagnosis, meaning they have other clinically apparent psychiatric illnesses such as depression or manic-depression that require medication. Other people might need antidepressants to help lift them from depression and help stop the demons screaming inside their heads.

Further, it may help those who have gotten off addictive drugs to understand that, at some point in their lives, they may have to take controlled substance drugs for medical reasons such as for pain after surgery. This is not a death sentence, but needs to be treated carefully by the health professional and the patient. The patient should be given no more of the drug than is absolutely necessary. And probably the best thing to do is to treat the experience as if it were a relapse. Assume that the patient will lose control of the decision to use or not to use the drug excessively. In other words, it's a controlled relapse, not a drug-seeking behavior.

Also, if you have a dependency, find a physician who understands addiction. You also need a pharmacist who understands addiction. For example, if you need an over-the-counter cold preparation, the pharmacist can help you choose one that is safer for you.

We need to remember, too, that once someone has been addicted, they're not immune from becoming addicted to other substances. This includes alcohol, even if they've never been alcoholic. It's often tough for people to accept that alcohol is risky. But once they've been addicted to a mood-altering substance and they have the brain chemistry that predisposes them to dependency, they're at risk.

The use of alcohol can lead to drug relapse. Alcohol can lower their inhibitions and they may decide to "use" again. It's also common to switch addictions from pills to alcohol, or vice versa.

Recovering individuals also should know about relapse counseling. This involves teaching the recovering person to recognize the early warning signals of impending relapse. Relapse is not just suddenly picking up a pill and taking it. Relapse is a long path of events; individuals can usually identify the sorts of things that lead them in a downward spiral toward relapse. For example, someone might start feeling anxious and start acting it out sexually, spending money, or being nasty with people. These may be warning signs that they need to get back to support meetings and talk to people. They're starting to isolate, which is a setup for relapse.

5

Support for Families

For every man or woman who suffers with addiction, at least five or six others are suffering also, often deeply. These are family members and close friends who anguish over seeing a loved one self-destruct with powerful prescription drugs. Addiction is a family disease—it affects everyone in the circle of family and friends. No one escapes the pain and the chaos. All too often, children bear emotional scars for life as a result of being raised in a home with an addicted parent; however, family members can take actions that may help their loved one. And there are actions that family members can take to ease their own pain.

Addiction Affects the Entire Family

All too often, family and friends see the addict as being the only one with the problem. But the drug abuser's behavior takes an emotional toll on everyone around him or her. Without insights and understanding, loved ones also spiral downward, deeper into the addiction trap.

If you have an addict in your family, you already know the pain and despair that addiction brings. Many families are ashamed about having an addict in the family—what will friends and relatives think? Living in the midst of addiction produces a range of other painful emotions—confusion, anxiety, and often depression.

Experts describe addiction as causing a form of "insanity," or emotional chaos, within a family. When the chemical of choice is a prescription drug, this insanity is intensified. Family members are further confused. At first, they believe their loved one must need the drug. Then, gradually, they question the way the addict is abusing the drug. They wonder if the doctor is aware of this abuse. If so, why does the physician continue to prescribe?

Furthermore, these drugs are not coming from a shadowy street dealer—in many cases, they're being prescribed by health professionals. Even though we know the addict is ultimately responsible, the family questions how a health-care system that heals us and saves lives can be the same system administering a drug that contributes to the destruction of their loved one.

The Toll of Addiction

"Drug abuse leads to violence, separation of parents and children, loss of jobs, feelings of hopelessness, serious money problems, single parenthood, anxiety over child-care needs, bad relationships, and emotional and behavioral difficulties in children. Many drug abusers end up in prison or jail. Sometimes they steal property to get money for drugs; or, often, they will commit crimes while 'high' on drugs."

—National Institutes for Health

Enabling the Addict

Those of us who have lived with addiction have seen its ravages in the form of family arguments, ruined holidays, legal problems, job loss, financial problems, traffic tickets, and worse—traffic accidents. Indeed, feeling powerless to stop someone you love from destroying himself or herself is an extremely painful experience. Many of us, with only the best of intentions, try to help, try to save our loved one from harm's way. But families, operating out of simple love and concern, often do the wrong thing because they do not understand the dynamics of addiction. Families and friends often *enable* the addict. Enabling involves rescuing or doing for someone what he or she should be doing himself or herself.

Levels of Enabling

Family and friends enable anytime they try to minimize the consequences of the addict's behavior. There are two stages of enabling—*innocent* and *desperate.*

In the *innocent phase* of enabling, family members think the person is just going through a little difficulty in his or her life, and so they try to "cover up" the consequences. An example of this might be paying the fine for a traffic accident, rather than addressing the underlying cause of the accident. The enabler may say, "Well, this is our beloved Jeff or our beloved Mary, who can't possibly be an addict like those people who live on the other side of the tracks."

In the *desperate phase,* the family finally realizes, because of the continuing consequences, that a loved one has a true addiction problem. They are so horrified that they actually step up the enabling process because they don't want the worst consequences to come about, such as a family member going to jail or losing a job. So they actually go into high gear enabling the problem, paying rent or paying medical expenses that may arise from the addiction.

Jill's Story
Learning to Not Enable

My twenty-three-year-old daughter Laura had originally been prescribed painkillers for legitimate chronic pain, but she increased the dosages and began a destructive, five-year bout with addiction. In hindsight, I realize our entire family enabled Laura.

Fortunately, she is in recovery now. I used to say her addiction was like seeing her on a speeding train heading toward a brick wall, and I could do nothing to stop it. It was so painful to see her destroying herself. In the beginning, we tried to help her, but we really were enabling her. For example, on three separate occasions, we set her up in an apartment. We helped her find each apartment and paid the deposits and first month's rent. We always thought Laura would get on her feet and be responsible. But she didn't. When she didn't pay the rent, the landlords would come looking for us.

Laura was a young woman who had never caused us problems or been in trouble. But as an addict, she was a different person altogether. We were exasperated. One doctor told us she was an addict, but we didn't believe it. We knew she needed pain medications, which had been prescribed by a doctor, so we were slow to believe she had an addiction problem.

At one point, Laura's grandmother took her into her home. Laura stole pain pills from her grandfather, who was quite ill at the time. She also caused a lot of damage to the house. She was high on pills and forgot to turn off the water in the bathtub; it overflowed and caused part of the ceiling to collapse. She also stole money from her father and me. One night she ran up a $1,000 phone bill, talking to a "psychic" on a 900 phone line all night. The chaos was ongoing.

Finally, we realized that the more we were helping Laura, the more she was failing. We had to quit supporting her. It was very difficult to stop rescuing her, but we did. However, we did not abandon her. We always told her we loved her, and that she could always call us collect, and that we would always be there to help her when she was ready to get help. We have a strong faith in God, and came to believe that only He could show her the way. Fortunately, she found the way and is now clean and sober.

Today, my advice for other families is not to rescue or enable the addict in your family. Ask yourself: Is what I'm doing helping matters or making them worse? But always let them know you will help them when they're ready to help themselves. Understand that addicts can't recover on their own. It's as if they've fallen into a well with moss-covered sides, and they can't get a grip to pull themselves up. To recover, they must reach out and ask for help. But, until they're ready, always let them know that you love them and that your heart is open.

Detach with Love

So, if it is not constructive to rescue the addict and he or she steadfastly refuses to get into treatment, what can you do? The theory behind the twelve-step support programs is to *detach* from the addict. This doesn't mean you stop loving the person. It doesn't mean abandoning the person or not being supportive if he or she decides to get help. It means "detaching with love" and stopping the game of rescue. The Al-Anon literature says, "detachment is neither kind nor unkind. It does not imply judgment or condemnation of the person or situation from which we are detaching. It is simply a means that allows us to separate ourselves from the adverse effects that another person's addiction can have upon our lives."

Too often, family and friends become obsessed with rescuing the addict. In the process, we teach addicts that they do not have to face the consequences of their actions—we'll be there to "pick up the pieces." As a result, we become "codependents," focused on the lives of the addicts rather than on taking care of ourselves. We succumb to the crises, the chaos, and the heartbreak.

Giving up the role of keeper or rescuer can be difficult, but in the end, we family members must come to the realization that even with all our rescuing, the addict has not changed. We must learn to take care of ourselves and seek help for our own emotional pain at seeing a loved one self-destruct. When family members get the focus back on themselves, the addict often realizes that the "game" is ending. Sometimes, he or she may give new consideration to taking responsibility for personal behaviors. Still, don't give up on an addict. Let the individual know that you are ready to help when he or she is ready to get help.

Molly's Story
Trying to Save a Marriage

I'm a special education teacher. I finally left my husband about a year ago. I had lived with his addiction to painkillers for nearly fourteen years. I loved him deeply and never wanted to divorce, but I could not allow any more emotional damage to be done to our children or me.

My husband, John, injured his spine in a car accident in 1989, when he was twenty-two. We were married in 1991. He had always had migraine headaches, and after the accident he had them more frequently. He also suffered with pain and eventually had back surgery to insert metal plates in his back. He was taking heavy doses of Demerol for pain. He was so drugged that sometimes he did not know me. He wouldn't be able to speak. He drooled. He is very tall—six foot five inches. At one point, he got down to 180 pounds. He was so skinny he looked like a prisoner of war. I didn't realize the problem was the drugs; I thought he had a problem in his brain. I videotaped his behavior to show his doctors.

We went to various doctors and specialists. At times, he would try to come off the medications, but his pain would be so severe that he would start the painkillers again.

It was about five years into the marriage that I discovered that he was getting additional drugs. I had sensed that something was not right—that there had to be another reason he was so affected by the drugs. I went to various pharmacies and got lists of the drugs he was taking. It turns out he was getting drugs from several doctors. I thought I could put a stop to this by canceling all our credit card accounts and closing the checking account so he wouldn't be able to buy drugs.

Then, I arranged for him to go to a treatment center. I dropped him off. He didn't even know it was a treatment facility. He stayed fourteen days. He came out sober and with no pain. No migraines. He went out and got a job with a construction company. Up until now, I had been the sole breadwinner. He was doing well. He changed jobs a couple of times, but managed to hold a job for about three years. We had our first child in 1997.

Then, in 1999, when I was eight months pregnant with our second child, I found Demerol in his overnight bag. I flushed them down the toilet. He was very angry with me. He said he was having pain again and that he needed the pain medication. He had gone to other doctors, whom I knew nothing about, to get the drugs.

What was to come was predictable. Soon, his behavior was changing. He was lethargic and was losing his motor control. I took him to a hospital, not totally understanding if he really had pain again or whether he was addicted. A nurse there told me he was addicted, but I defended him, saying he needed the medications for pain. Looking back, I realize I was in denial.

About two months later, he fell off a ladder at work and had to have knee surgery. He got more painkillers. He never went back to work after that. He receives disability income from the state.

As part of my faith, I do not believe in divorce, and I always believed I should not leave him just because he had been injured. This type of thinking kept me stuck for years. I knew deep down he was a good person. I just hoped I would get the real John back some day. I would always make excuses for him about why he didn't participate in family activities. He was so impaired that, eventually, the only task he was responsible for was doing the laundry.

When I finally realized the toll the addiction was taking on my children, I knew I had to leave. They deserved a stable environment. I finally gave him an ultimatum. I told him that if he didn't change, I was leaving with the kids. I've been gone two years now, and sadly, he hasn't changed. He lives with his mother. My kids are now eight and ten. We have stability in our lives now. They are happier and emotionally healthier. I finally see my husband differently now and I recognize the situation for what it is, but it took me a long time to get to that point.

Advice to Others: Don't discredit your own needs and tell yourself you're trying to help your addicted spouse. I thought I was helping John, but I was enabling him and all the while hurting myself and my children. I'll always remember the advice a therapist gave me. She said, "You can hope and pray that your husband recovers, but make decisions as though he never will."

Ten Ways a Family Members Can Help a Loved One with a Drug Problem

1. **Learn the facts about alcoholism and drug addiction.** Obtain information through counseling and/or open meetings of Alcoholics Anonymous or Narcotics Anonymous. Addiction thrives in an environment of ignorance and denial. Only when we understand the characteristics and dynamics of addiction can we begin to respond to its symptoms more effectively. Realizing that addiction is a progressive disease will assist family members to accept their loved one as having a disease rather than being a bad person. This comprehension goes a long way toward helping overcome the associated shame and guilt. No one is to blame.

   The problem is not caused by bad parenting or by any other family shortcoming. Attending an open Alcoholics Anonymous or Narcotics Anonymous meeting is important. You can also seek out family-support programs such as Al-Anon or Nar-Anon. These support groups help families see that they are not alone in their experience—that there are many other families involved in this struggle. Families will find a reason to be hopeful when they hear the riveting stories of recovery shared at these meetings.

2. **Don't rescue the alcoholic or addict. Let them experience the full consequence of their disease.** Unfortunately, it is extremely rare for anyone to be "loved" into recovery. Recovering people experience a "hitting bottom." This implies an accumulation of negative consequences related to drinking or drug use, which provides the necessary motivation and inspiration to initiate a recovery effort. It has been said that "truth" and "consequences" are the foundations of insight, and this holds true for addiction. Rescuing addicted persons from their consequences only ensures that more consequences must occur before the need for recovery is realized.

3. **Don't support the addiction by financially supporting the alcoholic or addict.** Money is the lifeblood of addiction. Financial support can be provided in many ways, and they all serve to prolong the arrival of consequences. Buying groceries, paying for a car repair, loaning money, paying rent, and paying court fines are all examples of contributing to the continuation of alcohol or drug use. Family members with the best of intentions almost always give money, but it always serves to enable the alcoholic or addict to avoid the natural and necessary consequences of addiction. Many addicts recover simply because they could not get money to buy drugs. Consequently, they experience withdrawal symptoms and often seek help.

4. **Don't analyze the loved one's drinking or drug use. Don't try to figure it out or look for underlying causes.** There are no underlying causes. Addiction is a disease. Looking for underlying causes is a waste of time and energy and usually ends up with some type of blame focused on the family or others. This "paralysis by analysis" is a common manipula-

tion by the disease of addiction that distracts everyone from the important issue of the illness itself.

5. **Don't make idle threats. Say what you mean, and mean what you say.** Words only marginally impact the alcoholic or addict. Actions speak louder than words when it comes to addiction. Threats are as meaningless as the promises made by the addicted person.

6. **Don't extract promises. A person with an addiction cannot keep promises.** This is not because they don't intend to, but rather because they are powerless to consistently act upon their commitments. Extracting a promise is a waste of time and only serves to increase the anger toward the loved one.

7. **Don't preach or lecture. The addicted person easily discounts preaching and lecturing.** A sick person is not motivated to take positive action through guilt or intimidation. If an alcoholic or addict could be "talked into" getting sober, many more people would get sober.

8. **Avoid the reactions of pity and anger. These emotions create a painful rollercoaster ride for the loved one.** The level of anger you feel toward an addicted loved one will be replaced by the same level (or more) of pity for the loved one once your anger subsides. This teeter-totter is a common experience for family members—they get angry over a situation, make threats or initiate consequences, and then backtrack from those decisions once the anger fades and is replaced by pity. The family then does not follow through on their decision not to enable.

9. **Don't accommodate the disease.** Addiction is a subtle foe. It will infiltrate a family's home, lifestyle, and attitudes in ways that can go unnoticed by the

family. As the disease progresses within the family system, the family will unknowingly accommodate its presence. Examples of accommodation include locking up valuables, not inviting guests for fear that the alcoholic or addict might embarrass them, adjusting one's work schedule to be home with the addict or alcoholic, and planning one's day around events involving the alcoholic or addict. (A spouse confided that she would set her alarm to get up and pick her husband up from the bar.)

10. **Focus on your life and responsibilities.** Family members must identify areas of their lives that have been neglected due to their focus on, or even obsession with, the addict or alcoholic. Other family members, hobbies, job, and health, for example, often take a backseat to the needs of the addict or alcoholic and the inevitable crisis of addiction. Turning attention away from the addict and focusing on other personal areas of one's life is empowering and helpful to all concerned.

Source: Ed Hughes, Executive Director, The Counseling Center Inc., www.thecounselingcenter.org.

What Is a Family Intervention?

In the best-case scenario, the one who's struggling with addiction will decide to seek treatment, but this doesn't always happen. In this case, you may wish to consider an *intervention.* An intervention is a planned event in which the person who is chemically dependent is confronted by family and friends in an effort to get him or her into treatment immediately. An intervention may be informal or structured.

Informal Intervention

In an *informal intervention,* a family member or friend, or possibly a therapist acting on behalf of the family, may confront the individual. Bruce Cotter is a professional interventionist who works with addicts on a one-to-one basis.

Having done interventions in which a group confronts an individual, he now prefers to work alone. "People I work with are scared, angry, confused, and paranoid. They're despairing, they're hurting, and they feel guilty. So, I find I can work more effectively with them alone, rather than confronting them with a group."

Cotter cites an example of working with a young man, Robert, from the Midwest. "When I met with the family, I could see how angry they were at their son. I don't think it would have been good to have them there for the intervention. Instead, I met alone with him at 6 o'clock in the morning at a motel. We sat and talked for almost three hours. He spit out a lot of stuff that he wanted to say, that he probably never would have stated in front of his family. Plus, I have credentials as a therapist, but I'm also a recovering addict, so I could assure Robert that I knew what he was going through."

In the course of working with an individual, Cotter wants the addict to *choose* treatment, not be talked into it. "The worst thing you can do is tell an addict what to do. They won't buy it. I want them to make the decision to seek treatment and then I support their decision. They already know they don't want to continue living the way they are, but they are afraid of giving up their drug of choice."

When Cotter is hired to do an intervention, he accompanies an individual to the treatment center. He has all transportation arranged—cars and plane tickets if necessary. He stays with the patient throughout the admission process at the treatment center. Then, a couple of weeks later, Cotter returns to the treatment center to check on the patient and offer his continued support. He also designs an aftercare program of support to be implemented upon the patient's release from a treatment center.

Cotter's services represent one style of informal intervention. If your budget won't cover such extensive involvement, including travel, help is still available. Many therapists and interventionists offer a range of services that may be tailored to fit your needs and budget.

Structured Intervention

A *structured intervention* involves family and friends, and sometimes a counselor. In either case, if the meeting concludes successfully, the individual is driven directly to the waiting treatment facility.

The intervention team is commonly made up of a group of three to eight family members and friends. Each team member needs to make a commitment to learn about the dynamics of addiction and how to intervene properly. This is important since each family member and friend usually has a different idea of what is right. It often helps to have a professional interventionist or therapist help plan and carry out the intervention.

Organizing the Intervention Team

Once assembled, the intervention team can discuss in detail their experiences of the negative consequences with the addict. This is often an eye-opening process because different family members and friends will have had different experiences with the addict; it may be quite a revelation to them to realize how they were involved in enabling. The team should also choose a chairperson and a "detail person," someone who will take care of all the little things about getting ready to get the addict into treatment.

Taking Care of Details

The team members need to plan ways to counter each objection the addict may have about entering treatment. "They need to be prepared for such objections as 'I can't take time off from my job,' in which case the family will have already talked to the employer in advance, without the addicts knowledge," states Jeff Jay, an interventionist and coauthor of *Love First: A New Approach to Intervention for Alcoholism and Drug Addiction*.

For someone who lives alone, the objection to going into treatment might be, "Who's going to take care of my dog?" It's important that the team has excellent answers to these objections. According to Jay, "You will never see an addict who is more shocked than when a team member says to him, 'We know how much your dog Spot likes Uncle Roger, and Roger has agreed to take Spot while you're in treatment. In fact, we're ready to take him over to Roger's house right now.' This kind of preparedness usually causes the addict's jaw to drop. They're saying to themselves, 'These people have thought of everything! Now is the time for me to get help.' "

Another important matter is to determine what treatment center the person will be going to. Will insurance cover it or not? The detail person needs to keep track of all this.

Carrying Out the Intervention

When the actual intervention takes place, experts say it's best to have it in a place outside the addict's home. The home of a team member is a good choice. Intervention should be done only when the person is sober, so this often means doing it early in the morning. "It's important to have the most important people in their life there. For example, if it's an adult male, I often try to have his mother walk right up to him, give him a hug, and say, 'Honey, we need to talk.' She may guide him over to the couch and everybody sits down," explains Jay.

He also recommends that the intervention be very tightly scripted, so rather than having people talk off the top of their heads, they actually take turns reading a letter to the addict. "I like to see the letters open up with very loving statements, which is often very surprising to the addict. This is a 180-degree difference from what they're expecting to hear. When the intervention is taking place, the last thing that the addict expects to hear is people telling them what a great person they are and how important they've been in that person's life. They expect to be beaten over the head. So what we do is, we put a different twist on it and this kind of destabilizes the addict and gets them ready to hear more.

"For example, a letter to me when I was in my addiction was, 'Dear Jeff: I love you, I care about you, and when I was going through a divorce five years ago, you were the one who was there for me. You're the one I could always count on to speak to, and you gave me such good counsel and support that I couldn't have made it without you. Now I see that you're going through difficulty and I am going to be there for you.' After they tell the addict how important they've been, their letter can explain, 'Ive taken some time to learn about alcoholism and drug addiction, and I understand that you have a medical problem. It's not a character issue. It's not a willpower issue. It's really a medical issue and I want you to get medical help for it.' "

Setting Up an Intervention

Interventions must be well organized. You may be able to find a therapist, who has experience with interventions, to help your family. You can also go online and find professional intervention services that will send an interventionist to you.

Next in their letters, the intervention group should move into a "fact reporting" phase in which they list the reasons why the addiction is causing problems. This should include no judgment, no blame, no anger. Just the facts. Then, in closing their letters, each member can reiterate love and concern and ask the addict to get treatment at a very specific treatment center right now. Today.

Joni's Story
A Brother's Intervention

I felt we had to do something to help my brother Jerry, age 40, with his addiction. I knew I would always feel bad if we didn't try. I organized a team of ten of us, including family, friends, and colleagues. We prepared for about two months. I read everything I could find about interventions. We also hired a professional interventionist to guide us.

The day we did the intervention, Jerry was invited to a friend's house, where we were all waiting. He was rather shocked to see us all there, especially since several of us had flown in from out of town. But, the second he saw us, he knew what was up. He was angry at first, but we'd all been told to expect this, so we did not let his anger dissuade us. We all talked to him, telling him how his addiction had affected him and us; we also stressed how much we loved him and wanted him well.

He tried to make an excuse—that he had to go home and pack. We told him his suitcase had already been packed by his wife; she had brought it over ahead of time. When he insisted that he be able to go home and shower, my other brother went with him. He asked us, "Are you afraid I'll run?" We all said, "Yes." He took a shower, returned, and my other brother and I took him to the treatment center. He completed treatment and has remained in recovery for several years now.

Looking back, I feel really good about what we did. We helped save his life. So, we had a good outcome, but it wasn't easy. It was a very emotionally taxing experience. It was scary, too, because we didn't know if we would succeed.

My advice to others who are considering an intervention: Do it. You will always know you tried. I also suggest educating yourself about interventions and being well organized. It's good to have the help of an interventionist or a counselor who understands how interventions are carried out and can guide you. These professionals can be objective, less emotional, whereas we family members are very emotional and not objective.

Paula's Story
Getting Help for Yourself

I lost my 28-year-old brother, Ray, to his drug addiction. He abused painkillers for years and ultimately died of an accidental overdose. My family really tried to help him, but in hindsight I realize that we were not informed about addiction. For example, I didn't know that it would be very difficult for him to quit drugs cold turkey. I also thought he took pills because he just liked getting high. In reality, of course, he was using pills to numb emotional pain.

I remember trying to help in ways that didn't help. For instance, I called more than one of his doctors to report that he was abusing the drugs they had prescribed. But as you might guess, my calls had no effect on the real problem. Another time, my parents and I even went to court and tried to have my brother committed to a treatment center; however, the law required us to prove that he was mentally ill and dangerous, which we could not prove. The judge dismissed the case, and my brother was furious with us, further inflaming the family ties.

Yet another time, we tried to convince Ray to voluntarily enter a treatment facility. My parents and I were willing to cover the costs. He reluctantly agreed to visit the treatment center with us. Once there, we spoke with a social worker. Ray was high on pills at the time of the visit and was belligerent to say the least. Finally, when we realized he would not agree to entering the rehab program, I recall the social worker telling us, "Go to a family support meeting such as Al-Anon or Nar-Anon, the sister organization to Narcotics Anonymous. If he won't get help for himself, get help for yourself."

I dismissed the suggestion, saying to myself that my brother was the one with the problem—not us. In hindsight, I realize how much we could have benefited from support. We needed help in coping with our own emotional pain and perhaps we could have learned about addiction and ways we might have been able to better help Ray.

Taking Care of Yourself

Interventions work well for many families. However, they don't always result in a loved one getting treatment.

Remember that addiction is a progressive disease—it gets worse if it is not brought under control. So, if your loved one will not agree to get professional help, get help for yourself. You're hurting, too. Seek emotional support. Consider finding a therapist in your area who is experienced in addiction issues, and look into support groups, such as Nar-Anon for families. Learn all you can about addiction. The more educated you are, the more prepared you'll be to help your loved yourself and your loved one.

6

Pain Management and Addiction

It is estimated that 20 percent of Americans suffer from chronic pain. Nearly three-fourths of this group report that pain interferes with daily activities, and about two-thirds of those with chronic pain take pain medication daily. The major causes of pain are headaches, back pain, arthritis, and cancer. Many causes of pain are related to aging, and most chronic pain sufferers are middle age or older.

Most people who are using painkillers for legitimate pain are using their medications as directed. However, those who abuse narcotic painkillers make up the largest group of prescription drug abusers in the United States. Between 1992 and 2002, prescriptions for pain pills increased 222 percent.

Risk of Addiction from Pain Treatment

According to the American Pain Society, the incidence of addiction is 3 percent among patients who are treated for legitimate chronic pain and have no history of drug abuse; these are patients who use pain medications as directed and who are evaluated regularly by their prescribing physicians. According to the study, these patients are using medications to ease their pain rather than to alter their mood.

However, some pain specialists say that they see a great number of people who are taking opioids for pain and become addicted. Edward Covington, M.D., is a pain specialist at the Cleveland Clinic. "In our chronic pain rehabilitation program, a little over 30 percent have an active addictive disorder."

From Treatment to Addiction

How do legitimate pain patients get themselves into trouble with pain medications? Problems may occur if patients are not honest with themselves and their physician. For example, a problem with addiction may arise if a patient's chronic pain still exists, but he or she starts using opioids to treat new or preexisting problems with anxiety, depression, sleep disorders, or adverse social or economic problems.

Other warning signs that you may be abusing pain medications include:

- You increase the number of pills you take.
- You go to different doctors to get more drugs.
- You mix alcohol with drugs to increase their effect.
- Your loved ones start expressing concern over your use of painkillers.

It's important for patients to keep their doctors informed of any of these warning signs. The physician may be able to help a patient avoid sliding deeper into addiction. For example, the patient may need help with coping skills and can be referred to a therapist. Or, the patient may need other medications that are nonopioid. In the case of depression, antidepressants would be the preferred medication rather than having the patient take increased doses of opioids.

Q & A with Pain Specialist Edward Covington, M.D.

Pain specialists are neurologists, physiologists, psychiatrists, nurses, and other specialists who are trained in pain management. According to pain specialists, treating chronic, nonmalignant pain can be complicated because the needs of those who suffer with it are diverse.

- **What type of patients do you see as a pain specialist?** Most patients who see pain specialists are those who have chronic, non-cancer-related pain. Probably over 60 percent have spine-related pain. The second most common pain I see is that from fibromyalgia or migraine headaches. The third largest group would be those with pain from arthritis or nerve damage.

- **What do you do when a pain patient becomes addicted?** Well, first, we don't withhold pain treatment from someone who has become addicted; however, we try to encourage the person to get into recovery. If you have an active addiction disorder and a chronic pain problem, probably anything we do for the person will fail until the addiction is brought under control.

  Keep in mind, we do see a condition known as "pseudo-addiction." This involves a situation in which a person is not receiving enough opioids for their pain and they exhibit "drug behavior," much like an addict. However, once we treat them with additional opioids, they become perfectly normal patients and do fine.

- **What should people do if they need surgery and pain management, but they are in recovery from addiction to alcohol or pain pills?** First, the patient should tell his or her surgeon and anesthesiologist about their history of addiction. After surgery, the surgeon should wean the patient off painkillers as soon as possible. We also encourage these patients to attend recovery meetings.

  We may suggest that the patient give their painkillers to a spouse or a relative, instructing them to give the patient their medications and give them only as directed. It's not right to ask a person in recovery to walk around all day with a bottle of Percocets in his pocket. I don't think I have seen an addict in recovery fail at managing postoperative pain when they developed a strategy with their doctors. The problem arises when the patient keeps their drug abuse a secret from the doctor; this may lead to doctor shopping or acquiring more drugs illegally.

- **Do you think doctors should have pain patients sign "pain contracts"?** Yes, they should. A pain contract shows that the patient has been told about the risks of addiction. This makes the patient more aware of potential risk, and it usually frees the doctor up to treat the pain more aggressively since he or she knows that the patient has been informed.

  A contract also informs the patient of side effects. And a pain contract gives the doctor the right to speak to family members and pharmacists. A family member may have a better sense of when someone is abusing opioids than the patient does.

- **How can pain patients monitor themselves to help prevent them from sliding into addiction?** The simplest thing people can do is remind themselves that an addictive disorder is a disease, and a disease does not make you get well. If you're taking opioids and your pain is less and your function is better, chances are good that you're not in trouble. However, if you've increased your dosages, you're still having pain, and you have a poor degree of function, then it's likely that the opioids have become more of a liability than an asset.

  There are other signals, too. You might be in trouble if you find yourself preoccupied with your pills, you can't seem to control how many you take, and you run out of them early. And of course, if you take increased dosages and continue to do so in spite of the problems it brings into your life, you have probably developed an addictive disorder.

- **What should a person do if his or her pain persists?** Many people are told that nothing more can be done for their pain, but this is not always the case. Chronic pain rehabilitation programs are not plentiful (there are about 3,000 pain specialists in the United States), but if you can find one, they can often help. In fact, pain clinics have a pretty high rate of success. Don't give up. Try a pain rehabilitation program.

Pain Is Often Undertreated

In spite of the growing public awareness that pain pills are highly abused in the United States, the fact is that legitimate pain is often undertreated. Federal guidelines estimate that as many as half of the millions of people who have surgery annually receive inadequate pain management for postsurgical pain. It's also estimated that as many as 80 percent of cancer patients do not receive adequate medication for pain.

Fear of Addiction

One of the main barriers to effective pain management is fear of addiction—by both patients and health professionals. "In the past few years we've tried to focus on improving pain management because we know that for the past several decades pain has not been well controlled," states Betty R. Ferrell, R.N., Ph.D., an associate research scientist on pain management at City of Hope National Medical Center, Duarte, California. "When we see patients who are afraid to take the pain medication, we explain the difference between drug addiction and physiological dependence. In the latter case, if the patient should eventually come off the pain medication, it would be done gradually with medical supervision; otherwise, the patient would have withdrawal."

High-profile cases also create myths about addiction, explains Ferrell. "When we hear about a celebrity who's addicted to prescription drugs, we think we're all candidates for such addiction; however, these celebrities often have a history of alcoholism or addiction. And it is those patients who do have a history of substance abuse who can become addicted to their medication."

Undereducated Physicians

Studies indicate that medical students lack pain management training. In one study, reported by the *Journal of the American Board of Family Practice*, 88 percent of the doctors surveyed stated that their training in pain management was poor. Seventy-three percent stated their residency training was fair or poor.

To avoid problems with addiction, pain management experts stress the importance of proper evaluation of patients; such evaluation may determine whether a patient has underlying emotional problems (such as depression or anxiety) that may predispose him or her to escalating doses and becoming addicted. Experts also stress the importance of continued reevaluation of patients to detect signs of addiction.

Doctors' Concerns about Being Investigated

Creating public awareness about the abuse of prescription drugs, especially painkillers, creates serious concerns for health professionals who deal in pain management. Media coverage about the abuse of painkillers may cause doctors to decrease the amount of painkillers they prescribe. Doctors often have concerns that they may come under scrutiny and their medical licenses may be at risk if they appear to be prescribing too many controlled substances, even though some patients may need ongoing, high dosages of painkillers to combat pain.

"Reluctance to prescribe opioids for intractable pain can often be attributed to physicians' perceptions that they will be investigated for violation of laws governing controlled substances," states David Joranson, senior scientist and director for policy studies with the Pain Research Group at the University of Wisconsin. "These laws and regulations amount to legal barriers to pain management. The medical use of controlled substances can provide great improvements in the quality of life for millions of people with debilitating medical conditions."

Joranson acknowledges the need for diversion control; however, he also stresses the importance of not restricting legitimate patients' access to narcotics for pain. "It is essential that we evaluate the barriers to effective pain relief. It's important to understand that opioid analgesics are the mainstay in the treatment of acute pain. Consumers should talk to caregivers if pain is not being treated sufficiently."

Pain Is Treatable

An important thing for consumers to know is this: Pain relief is available. Widely accepted medical treatment for cancer pain shows a success rate of 70 to 90 percent, if a patient's physician follows a standard, accepted guideline for pain control. Similarly, if appropriate guidelines are followed for the treatment of acute pain, such as postoperative pain in hospital settings, the success rate for treatment is 90 to 95 percent. As mentioned earlier, if a patient has any concerns that he or she is losing control and becoming addicted, the patient needs to be honest about this with his or her physician.

Barriers to Effective Pain Management

Problems Related to Patients

- Reluctance to report pain
- Concern about distracting physicians from treatment of the underlying disease
- Fear that pain means the disease is worse
- Concern about not being a "good" patient
- Reluctance to take pain medications
- Fear of addiction or being thought of as an addict
- Worries about unmanageable side effects
- Concern about becoming tolerant to pain medications

Problems Related to Health Professionals

- Inadequate knowledge of pain management
- Poor assessment of pain
- Concern about regulation of controlled substances
- Fear of patient addiction
- Concern about side effects of analgesics
- Concern about patients becoming tolerant to analgesics

Problems Related to the Health-Care System

- Low priority given to cancer pain treatment
- Inadequate reimbursement
- Restrictive regulation of controlled substances
- Availability of treatment or access to treatment

7

Seniors: At Risk for Drug Misuse and Addiction

The incidence of drug abuse among seniors is, in part, a result of their exposure to multiple drugs. People sixty-five and older make up 13 percent of the U.S. population, yet they take 30 percent of all prescription drugs sold in the United States. It is not unusual for a senior patient to be taking ten to fifteen medications a year, five of them simultaneously at any given time. And seniors may be seeing multiple physicians, getting different medications from each doctor, but not discussing their other prescriptions with each doctor.

Each year, drug misuse among seniors accounts for more than 9 million adverse drug reactions and 245,000 hospitalizations. Twenty-five percent of nursing home admissions occur annually as a result of seniors' inability to use medicines safely. Furthermore, adverse drug events are the fifth leading cause of death among older people.

Adverse Drug Interactions

If care is not taken to see that drugs work safely together, the results can be harmful. Seniors are more prone to adverse drug reactions because they metabolize drugs differently than younger individuals do. As we grow older, normal changes in the body result in a decrease in the percentage of water and lean tissue and an increase in fat. Also, the kidneys and liver can begin to function less efficiently. These factors affect the time a drug stays in the body and the amount absorbed by body tissues.

Medications Potentially Harmful to Seniors

In the first national study of its kind, researchers at Harvard University first reported in 1994 that 28 percent of the nation's senior citizens—nearly 7 million people—were taking prescribed drugs considered dangerous to their health. Experts say the study only scratches the surface, that as many as one-half to two-thirds of senior citizens living in senior communities are being prescribed drugs that are doing them unnecessary harm. These drugs range from those that may cause dizziness to those that may increase the risk of bone marrow toxicity and cause dangerous fluid retention. For a list of these drugs, see Appendix B in the back of the book.

Sedatives Pose Risks

Which drugs pose the biggest risk factors for seniors? "Taking sedatives or sleeping pills is the most dangerous thing for elderly people," says Steffie Woolhandler, M.D., coauthor of the Harvard study. "The drugs don't wear off by morning, leaving seniors sleepy and confused and prone to falling and hip fractures." According to the Food and Drug Administration, 32,000 seniors suffer hip fractures annually as a result of falls associated with the adverse effects of tranquilizers or painkillers. If you have a relative in a nursing home, ask the staff once or twice a year for a medical review of all drugs being prescribed.

Woolhandler, a former professor at Harvard Medical School, attributes part of the problem of seniors taking potentially harmful drugs to physicians "misprescribing." The education for young physicians about drug use is abysmal. We do not do a very good job teaching medical students about drug therapy. Medical educators need to do a better job of teaching physicians about medications."

Addiction among Seniors

Approximately 17 percent of those sixty and older are affected by prescription drug abuse. Approximately 11 percent of women over the age of fifty-nine are addicted to psychoactive prescription drugs, according to Columbia University's National Center on Addiction and Substance Abuse. As part of its study on drug abuse in senior women, the center reviewed prescriptions for 13,000 mature women over a six-month period. The report concluded that half of the prescriptions for tranquilizers and sleeping pills should not have been given or should have been given for a shorter period of time.

Recognizing Addiction in Seniors

Addiction in seniors is usually less recognizable than that in younger individuals. Seniors often live alone, so family and friends may not notice the telltale signs of addiction. Seniors are often retired, so work-related problems don't show up; nor do they seem to get as many traffic citations for driving under the influence.

Symptoms of addiction in seniors may include: memory loss, depression, mood swings, irritability, inability to concentrate, and talk of suicide. Friends and relatives may view these symptoms as being part of the aging process. Unfortunately, physicians are often not experienced in diagnosing addiction in seniors. As part of the Columbia study on addiction in seniors, 400 doctors were asked to give their top five diagnoses in a hypothetical case in which a patient exhibited the symptoms of early-stage alcoholism. Less than 1 percent of the doctors mentioned alcoholism as a diagnosis. Ninety-three percent of the physicians listed depression as their top diagnosis.

Alcohol and Drug Combinations Increase Risks

Also, an estimated 10 percent of seniors drink heavily—twelve to twenty-one drinks per week; and they are poor at reporting alcohol use, often because they are ashamed of it. For example, when a sixty-two-year-old California woman fell and broke her hip, the hospital staff was unaware that she had been taking Valium, drinking wine, and had become chemically dependent. The combination of chemicals caused her fall. "On the fourth day after her hip surgery, she started having very serious withdrawal symptoms," says David Smith, M.D., former president of the American Society of Addiction Medicine. "It's a substantial problem in the elderly. Fifty percent of delirium in the elderly in hospitals is related to the side effects of prescription drugs." Confusion, slurred speech, and memory loss are also side effects.

Getting Treatment

Since substance abuse among seniors is grossly underdiagnosed, only a small percentage are referred to treatment. Other barriers to treatment are pessimism, shame, and denial. The senior and his or her family may fail to acknowledge the problem. And if the problem is acknowledged, elderly persons may question the value of getting sober at a time when they may believe they have only a few years left to live.

Finally, like many others, senior citizens often view addiction as a moral problem rather than as an illness to be diagnosed and treated. "Seniors are especially sensitive about this, and this attitude presents an obstacle to getting treatment," says Carol Colleran, of the Florida-based Hanley Center, a nationally recognized addiction treatment facility, which offers a program for older adults. "Seniors are usually very ashamed of their addiction problem and often get quite angry about any suggestion that they need help."

Accordingly, it's important that family members be supportive and help seniors understand that chemical dependency is an illness. "If you have diabetes, you take insulin. If you have high cholesterol, you take cholesterol-lowering medications," explains Colleran. "If you have an addiction, you need to get treatment for it, too." She offers the following advice for family members dealing with seniors who may have become chemically dependent:

- Don't try to reason with a person while he or she is under the influence of a drug.
- Avoid harsh confrontations. Be gentle in discussing problems.
- Avoid use of the term "drug addict," since this term carries a heavy stigma among seniors.
- Understand that throwing away pills won't help. An individual who is not ready to receive help will only replenish the supply.
- Be direct and be specific about your concerns for the individual. Let the person know your family is concerned about his or her well-being and that he or she is loved and cared for.

Will Insurance Pay for Seniors' Treatment?

As mentioned previously, the cost of addiction treatment may not be covered by insurance. In many cases, insurance companies or Medicare will pay for inpatient detox, which is considered a medical procedure; and Medicare will pay for medical costs for addiction-related injuries such as falls. However, Medicare does not usually pay for primary treatment for addiction.

On a positive note, seniors, overall, are more likely to complete a treatment program, once they enter it. Those who become chemically dependent late in life show the best response to treatment.

Avoiding Drug Misuse

If you are a senior or if you are a caregiver for a senior, what can you do to prevent dangerous drug misuse by an elderly person? One way to help is to get a medicine review. At least once a year (three times a year is better), put all medications in a bag and take them to a doctor or pharmacist and ask for a medicine review. Among the common problems discovered during medicine reviews are:

- Outdated medicines
- Inappropriate drug interactions
- Patient confusion over drugs with similar names
- Over/underutilization when the patient has not understood the instructions
- Pills "borrowed" from friends
- Duplicate prescriptions—from different doctors—with serious potential for overdose

A medicine review should be repeated whenever a new drug is added. If you have access to the Internet, you may go to a variety of sites that will do online checks for potential drug interactions. Do a keyword search for "drug checker" or "drug interaction checker." It's also recommended that you discuss drug regimens with your pharmacist and physician.

Questions to Ask about Your Medications

Just as it's important to get thorough medical checkups, it's also important to be well informed about your medications. When new medications are prescribed for you, ask your health professional whether the drug has any addiction potential. Inform the physician if you have any history of alcoholism or drug addiction or if you have any concerns about such drugs. In addition, the National Council on Patient Information and Education recommends that you ask the following questions about every drug that is prescribed for you:

1. What is the name of the medicine, and what is it for? Is this the brand name or the generic name?
2. Is the generic version of the medication available?
3. How and when do I take it—and for how long?
4. What foods, drinks, other medicines, dietary supplements, or activities should I avoid while taking this medication?
5. When should I expect the medication to begin to work, and how will I know if it is working? Are there any tests required with the medicine (for example, to check liver or kidney function)?
6. Are there any side effects? If so, what are they, and what do I do if they occur?
7. Will this drug work safely with the other prescription and nonprescription medications I am taking? Will it work safely with any dietary or herbal supplements I am taking?
8. Can I get a refill? If so, when?
9. How should I store this medication?
10. Is there any written information available about this medication?

Finally, it is helpful for senior citizens to have all medications filled at one pharmacy, where patient medication lists are maintained on a computer; the computer will call attention to any new drug that has the potential to interact negatively with other drugs. It's also important to safeguard against the tendency of seniors to take a drug indefinitely once it has been prescribed. If a medicine review is done every three months, for example, the physician can be asked if a specific drug is still needed.

Caution about Over-the-Counter Drugs

While senior citizens take three times the amount of drugs as the rest of the population, their use of over-the-counter medications is even greater. To many, drugs bought over the counter may seem harmless, compared to prescription drugs. However, the active ingredients in pills purchased over the counter can be harmful to seniors. "For example, some of the ingredients in over-the-counter sleep aids are potent and can cause confusion and delirium in senior citizens," states Myron Weiner, M.D., a geriatric psychiatrist and expert on medications and the elderly.

Weiner also warns that herbal potions may cause problems. "People tend to think these herbals are harmless since they're not really drugs, but the ingredients can be potent and cause negative interactions with other drugs. Patients need to check with their pharmacists or doctors to see if there is a danger of adverse interaction with other drugs being taken."

Part II

Obtaining Fraudulent Prescriptions

8

Diverting Drugs from Doctors

For many years, experts have reported that the majority of prescription drug diversions occur at doctors' offices, where patients are doctor shopping. They feign pain or illness to obtain drugs from multiple doctors.

Where does the physician's role fit into these scenarios? The American Medical Association (AMA) has adopted a "5-D physician classification" to explain why physicians, or other health professionals such as physician assistants and advanced nurse practitioners, might misprescribe. The five categories are: duped, dated, distracted, dishonest, and disabled.

Duped

Here, the physician is most vulnerable. Failing to detect deception, a physician may be duped into prescribing drugs for a dishonest patient. The scams used by the deceiving patient are limited only by the patient's creativity. A patient may feign backache, migraine headaches, or complain of any number of ailments. These patients usually request specific medications and show no interest in confirming a diagnosis or undertaking other forms of treatment.

Addicts often regard health professionals as "easy marks" due to their training, which is geared to helping people and delivering relief from pain. Given the right circumstances, any physician may be deceived.

Dated

The dated doctor fails to keep current with prescribing practices or knowledge about current drug abuse patterns. A physician might misprescribe psychoactive drugs because the data on which that prescription is based are obsolete. Also, a number of doctors acknowledge that many medical schools do not adequately teach how to prescribe controlled substances. And for years, the view that drug and alcohol abuse are moral, rather than medical, problems has resulted in the omission of these subjects from medical school course work.

A survey by the National Center on Addiction and Substance Abuse (CASA) at Columbia University discovered that only 19 percent of primary care physicians received training about prescription drug diversion in medical school, 39 percent reported having received training during their residencies, and 34 percent through continuing education.

The same CASA survey found that most physicians feel unprepared to diagnose substance abuse and lack confidence in the effectiveness of treatment. Only 20 percent of doctors considered themselves "very prepared" to diagnose alcoholism. Only 17 percent said they felt prepared to diagnose illegal drug use, and just 30 percent said they could diagnose prescription drug abuse. An even smaller number of doctors (4 percent) believed treatment programs for alcoholism are effective, and only 2 percent thought treatment was effective for illegal drug abuse.

While doctors describe themselves as being unprepared to diagnose and recommend treatment for addiction, the need among patients for this help is strong. The AMA reports that addiction disorders affect 20 to 50 percent of all hospitalized patients, 15 to 30 percent of patients seen in primary care physicians' offices, and up to 50 percent of patients with psychiatric illnesses. Unfortunately, many of these cases of addiction go undiagnosed; an early diagnosis and getting help could reduce a patient's chances of descending deep into an addiction.

Distracted

Some doctors may be distracted. Busy schedules may make them less attentive in their prescribing and record keeping. Because of this, they may be more willing to prescribe a drug without getting a thorough patient history.

Dishonest

According to the AMA, only 1 percent (approximately 5,000 to 7,000) of the nation's doctors fall into the dishonest category. These physicians, or so-called "script docs," are those who use their medical licenses to deal drugs. Even though only a very small percentage of health professionals are considered dishonest, this group of professionals has been known to illegally prescribe vast quantities of drugs.

A case involving a physician in Illinois demonstrates the damage one dishonest doctor can cause. The physician, along with sixteen other defendants, was arrested for diverting nearly 60,000 tablets of the prescription drug Dilaudid, a painkiller. The street value of the drug was nearly $17 million.

In Indiana, a physician was arrested after prescribing large amounts of Seconal, Percocet, Placidyl, Valium, and Fastin. Investigators estimate that only 5 percent of his practice was legitimate. His small waiting room was typically packed with up to twenty-five people, all waiting for bogus prescriptions. At one point, only two pharmacies were willing to fill the prescriptions he wrote. Both pharmacies were later closed down.

As one California Bureau of Narcotic Enforcement agent explained, "We talk to addicts who are informants, and they tell us which doctors they go to. The informants say, 'All you have to do is give the doctor some phony excuse. He just needs something to write down [as an illness], and he'll charge you $150 for it. You probably spend about five minutes there.' "

Disabled (Impaired)

The disabled physician misprescribes because of his or her own impairment, which may be mental illness or personal abuse of painkillers or sleeping pills. Several studies show that health professionals have a higher prevalence of substance abuse than the general population. According to a survey conducted by the American Medical Association, approximately 15 percent of all health professionals will have a drug or alcohol problem in the course of their careers.

One reason for this is health-care professionals having access to controlled substances, often making it relatively easy for them to divert and abuse medications to relieve stress or enhance alertness and performance. Alcohol ranks first among the substances most often misused by health professionals; narcotics rank second.

"If you're going to have a medical license, you should be drug tested," insists Robert L. DuPont, M.D., an addiction medicine physician and former director of the National Institute on Drug Abuse. "I don't understand a society that says we will test bus drivers for drug use, but we won't test surgeons."

Physician and Patient Responsibilities for Preventing Drug Abuse

Responsibilities of the Physician

- To have the patient's well-being as the primary concern
- To formulate a working diagnosis of the patient's problems based on the patient's history and by examination of the patient
- To order appropriate lab tests (or consultations with a specialist) to clarify a diagnosis
- To prescribe appropriate therapy (This assumes the physician is acting within his/her scope of expertise.)
- To monitor the effect of treatment, including the side effects or toxicity of any drugs prescribed
- To continue follow-up until the condition is relieved or the patient's care is assumed by another physician

Responsibilities of the Patient

- To seek medical attention for conditions that he or she believes a physician can cure or ameliorate
- To be truthful in relating historical information and to cooperate with the physical examination
- To tell physicians about all other physicians providing treatment and about all other medications being taken
- To obtain the lab tests or consultations requested by the physician
- To comply with the physician's instructions (This includes taking medications as prescribed.)
- To report symptoms accurately
- To follow through with appointments until discharged by the physician

9

Diverting Drugs from Pharmacies

Nearly 4 billion drug prescriptions are filled every year in the United States. Most of these prescriptions are dispensed from the 33,000 pharmacies operated by drugstore chains, supermarkets, and mass merchants. The balance of the prescriptions are filled in the 20,000 pharmacies that operate independently.

Next to doctor shopping, presenting forged prescriptions to pharmacies is one of the most common techniques used by those obtaining prescriptions fraudulently. Why do individuals take a chance at passing forged prescriptions? First, they are often motivated by an addiction that demands drugs. Also, the offense is often perceived by offenders as victimless—no one is really getting hurt. The chances of arrest are often minimal, and if they are apprehended, penalties are often minimal. Last, the practice can be lucrative if the offender is selling the drugs to others.

Fraudulent Prescriptions

Just as the medical professional is susceptible to the doctor shopper, pharmacies are vulnerable to the "pharmacy shopper." A variety of techniques are used to obtain drugs fraudulently from drugstores. Some people steal prescription pads from doctors' offices and forge the prescribers' signatures. Others may counterfeit prescriptions by making hundreds of copies of legitimate physicians' prescriptions and then forging prescribers' signatures. Yet others may pose as a physician or a member of a physician's office staff on the telephone.

Rob, 34, a businessman from the Midwest, became very adept at diverting controlled substances from pharmacies.

Rob, 34

Businessman

I was coming off a year's binge with cocaine. I had gone through several hundred thousand dollars' worth of coke. I lost my house, my friends, my job. I could no longer afford cocaine, so I went back to morphine and Demerol.

In the beginning of my drug seeking, I went to doctors' offices, feigning back ailments to get prescriptions. But a lot of doctors were suspicious and I didn't get what I wanted. I could get some prescriptions, but not for the heavy drugs I wanted or for the quantities I needed. I really wasn't quenching the habit that I had. So I eventually stole a prescription pad from one doctor's office; I got his DEA number, so I just wrote my own prescriptions for what I wanted. Eventually, I stole other pads from other doctors and hospitals. At one time, I had thirty to forty pads from different doctors.

I knew one doctor and one dentist who would give me a prescription, as a kickback, when I made an appointment with them. This, however, was the exception rather than the rule. I think I had hit about every pharmacy in the metropolitan area. I was worried about getting caught. But of all the prescriptions I got filled, I would say I got turned down only about 1 percent of the time. And I don't think I was that good at what I was doing. I just think some pharmacists didn't know what to do with a suspicious prescription. A few pharmacists just turned their heads. I was very comfortable going to some drugstores. I don't know if they just wanted the business or didn't want the hassle of reporting me. But I would go to their stores, often high on drugs. They had to have noticed.

My drug of choice was Demerol, which is synthetic morphine. On an average day, I was going through 1,500 milligrams of Demerol. The drug came in 50-milligram and 100-milligram tablets. A typical prescription for bad pain might be one 50-milligram tablet every four hours. So, I'd say a high prescribed dosage would be 300 milligrams a day. My habit was progressive, getting worse over time.

It was easy to get drugs. I would get one or two prescriptions a day. My preferred method of using was to inject it, so I would dissolve the tablets in saline solution. I was hauled to the hospital by ambulance several times for overdosing. My day-to-day life revolved around getting drugs. It was a miserable existence. I lied and cheated. I needed drugs more than food, companionship, or shelter. I looked like a cadaver. Everyone around me told me how sick I was and how I needed help. Unfortunately, I was the last one to realize it.

Eventually, I was arrested. In hindsight, I believe I wanted to get caught. I was crying out for help. In fact, toward the end of my drug spree, I was using my real name and address when I wrote my own prescriptions.

The day I was arrested, I had gone to the same pharmacy twice in one day to get prescriptions filled. The pharmacist had become suspicious. So, when he gave me the second prescription, he gave me only half the pills, explaining that he was out of them and that I'd have to come back for the second half. I thought it might be a setup, but I was also an addict, so I went back later for the second half. I even waited for thirty minutes.

The pharmacist had called the police and they came and arrested me. Initially I was terrified of what was going to happen to me, but at the same time I was relieved that things were coming to an end. On some level, I knew I was very sick and needed help. Anyone living the life I was can expect to sit down to a banquet of consequences. I was long overdue.

I faced a five-to-ten-year jail term, but I was lucky—I got probation. I'm now in recovery. I speak to recovery groups around town. I think very few people have an understanding of the scope of prescription drug abuse and addiction. My case was extreme, but a lot of others are abusing on a lesser level; they think it's okay because it's a prescription drug.

Theft from Pharmacies

As addiction rates have increased in the United States, so has the number of thefts, robberies, and burglaries. These crimes are being committed both "internally" and "externally."

Internal Theft

Today, more employees have access to pharmacies, increasing the possibility of diversion. These employees include pharmacy clerks and technicians, who may not be subject to background checks, and interns, who are pharmacy students. In many cases, store managers, who are not pharmacists, may also have access to pharmaceuticals.

"Many stores hire high school kids to work as pharmacy clerks, and some of them have opportunities to steal drugs," explains John Mudri, a former DEA diversion investigator who spent thirty years investigating the diversion of pharmaceuticals. Many of his investigations involved drugstores. "I've been told by many store managers that their biggest problem with theft is from store clerks." In one case, a Bradenton, Florida, teenager stole narcotics for two years before finally being arrested. "She would create bogus prescriptions for Vicodin and Lortab, and have her friends pick them up at the drive-through window."

As a result of such crimes, some chain pharmacies have developed security teams that work to prevent fraud and theft by employees. When employees are caught stealing drugs, they are fired and reported to law enforcement.

Like the rest of the population, a certain percentage of pharmacists may develop an addiction problem; they may be inclined to use prescription drugs rather than alcohol. And as

Reported Pharmacy Thefts Nationwide
January 1, 2001 - December 31, 2006
Armed Robberies and Night Break-Ins Only

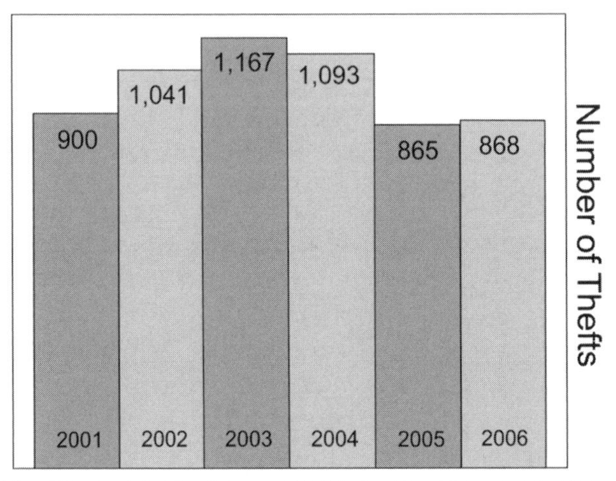

Office of Diversion Control, Drug Enforcement Administration, Office of Enforcement Operations, Pharmaceutical Investigations Section, Targeting and Analysis Unit - Drug Theft and Loss, 05/31/2007

mentioned earlier, about 1 percent of doctors in the nation are considered dishonest and likely to become involved in writing fraudulent prescriptions. Similarly, it's estimated that about 1 percent of pharmacists may be involved in the illegal dispensing of controlled substances.

External Theft

The last decade has seen an increase in the number of pharmacy robberies and thefts across the United States. Generally, the robberies are committed by individuals seeking drugs for their personal use; burglaries are often more sophisticated and usually result in the theft of a greater amount of controlled substances. The individuals committing such burglaries are typically involved in reselling the drugs. This is the assessment of the RxPatrol (Rx Pattern Analysis Tracking

Robberies and Other Losses), the nation's first information clearinghouse on crimes occurring in pharmacies, including robberies, thefts, fraud, employee theft, and cargo thefts. Founded in 2003, it is funded by the pharmaceutical company Purdue Pharma.

How does the program work? When pharmacy crimes occur, details of the crime are entered electronically into the Web site www.RxPatrol.com by law enforcement personnel, pharmacy personnel, or security professionals. The data are analyzed and disseminated to more than 2,500 drug diversion investigators daily.

Since its inception, the RxPatrol has documented nearly 4,400 cases of pharmacy crimes. How does the dissemination of this information help lead to arrests? "Many times we can help other communities identify suspects in robberies and burglaries by such things as their mode of operation, their descriptions, or streaming video taken by security cameras," according to Richard Conklin, a 29-year police veteran and a consultant to the RxPatrol. "Many of these suspects are serial robbers—they'll hit different counties and states. For example, we had one couple in Indiana who committed sixty-six robberies in four states."

The RxPatrol also uses sophisticated software to conduct crime trend analysis and vulnerability assessments for the pharmacy community. These reports offer guidance to pharmacies on how they can become aware about robbery trends and patterns and minimize their risk of theft-related crimes. For more information, visit Rxpatrol.com

Other Factors Affecting Diversion

Pressure for Profits

Some pharmacies may be under pressure to reach financial goals, making it more difficult for pharmacists to take time to investigate suspicious prescriptions. According to one pharmacist from the Midwest, "Many of these work scenarios are daunting. I once had a supervisor tell me, 'We pay you to type labels, not visit with customers.' A lot of pharmacists are concerned about this, especially once they have to start doing 200 to 400 scripts a day."

Depending on their staffing, pharmacists and technicians may not have the time to investigate all possible bogus prescriptions. If staffing is short, pharmacists may have to consider the degrees of alerts. For example, the alerts that pharmacists pay most attention to are those that deal with a patient receiving a new drug that is not compatible with another drug currently being taken; such medication incompatibilities can be life-threatening.

Pharmacists' Lack of Familiarity with Customers

In days past, pharmacists in smaller, neighborhood pharmacies were more likely to recognize regular customers. Anyone passing a suspicious prescription was fairly easily detected. Nowadays, larger pharmacies have larger customer bases, making it more difficult for pharmacists to recognize suspicious customers. Larger chain stores may also rotate pharmacists and use "floaters," employees who move from store to store; these employees would not be as familiar with the regular customers, making it more difficult for them to recognize the suspicious customers.

Rogue Internet Pharmacies

Within the past decade, the Internet has brought a new dimension to prescription drug diversion—it is now possible to buy controlled substances online. Unfortunately, many rogue pharmacies are not U.S. state–licensed pharmacies, and in many cases they are not pharmacies at all—they are sales operations based in foreign countries. Many of these sites do not require a doctor's prescription. In 2007, the National Center on Addiction and Substance Abuse (CASA) at Columbia University completed 210 hours of online research, documenting the presence of Internet sites that dispense prescription drugs, including painkillers. The researchers found 187 sites that were selling controlled substances, and 84 percent of these sites did not require a prescription.

However, purchasing drugs from these sites poses numerous dangers, according to the Food and Drug Administration (FDA). They say some drugs sold online:

- Are fake—they don't contain ingredients they claim to
- Are too strong or too weak
- Have dangerous ingredients
- Have expired—the drugs are old
- Are not FDA approved
- Are not made using safe standards
- Are not labeled, stored, and shipped correctly
- Are not safe to use with other medications

It is also likely that these Internet pharmacies will not protect your personal information.

A safe Web site would be located in the United States and be licensed by the state board of pharmacy in the state in which it operates. It would also require a licensed doctor's prescription and have a licensed pharmacist available to answer questions.

Policing Internet Drug Sales: Not an Easy Task

"Cyberspace is ideally suited to illicit drug transactions, creating a complex challenge for law enforcement, policy makers, and the general public," states Mathea Falco, President of Drug Strategies, a research institute dedicated to promoting effective approaches for dealing with substance abuse. Falco's testimony before Congress in 2006 reflects the difficulty in halting illegal drug sales online. "Businesses wishing to circumvent the U.S. Controlled Substances Act may do so by establishing multiple Web sites, in multiple countries, under multiple online identities. Many of the Web sites selling drugs are hosted outside the United States, and drug suppliers guarantee (and actually do) replace any drugs intercepted by U.S. Customs. Recent studies indicate that Russia, Ukraine, and the South Asian countries are emerging as the key locations for drug sales Web sites.

"For example, a 'no-prescription Web site' can be physically located on a computer in Uzbekistan, registered to a business address in Mexico, ship its drugs from Pakistan, and deposit payments to a Cayman Island bank. All the while, the owner resides in Miami. Importantly, all the links in this online enterprise can be quickly dismantled and resurrected under a new set of virtual identities."

Combating Rogue Internet Pharmacies

The researchers who wrote the CASA report on Internet drug sales make the following recommendations for combating rogue pharmacies:

- Congress should clarify federal law to prohibit the sale or purchase of prescription drugs online without an original copy of a prescription written by a DEA-certified physician.
- Online pharmacies should be certified in order to identify noncertified sites as illegal.
- Internet search engines should provide warnings that the sale and purchase of drugs from unlicensed pharmacies is illegal; sites that are not legal should be blocked.
- The federal government should provide online public service announcements about the dangers and illegality of buying drugs from noncertified sites.
- The DEA, credit card companies, and money order issuers should collaborate to restrict purchases of drugs from nonlicensed sellers.
- Postal and shipping service personnel should be trained to spot pharmaceutical trafficking.
- The State Department should encourage and assist foreign governments to crack down on illegal Internet drug sites.

Finally, the CASA report suggests that the federal government, Internet search providers, shippers, financial institutions, and nonprofit organizations create a national clearinghouse to identify and shut down illegal Internet pharmacies.

Part III

Efforts to Curb Drug Abuse

10

Prescription Drug Monitoring Programs

If you are a person addicted to prescription drugs, you're likely already aware of the numerous ways to obtain controlled substances from doctors and pharmacies. If you are a relative or a friend of an addicted person, you have no doubt questioned how prescription drugs can be obtained seemingly with little effort.

Today, many states are making efforts to curb the abuse of prescription drugs with prescription monitoring programs (PMPs). These programs identify individuals who receive excessive amounts of controlled substances such as painkillers, tranquilizers, or stimulants.

Model State Drug Laws

Most prescription monitoring programs are the result of the 1992 President's Commission on Model State Drug Laws, which was formed to help states develop laws to fight the drug crisis in America. These laws were first made available in January 1994 for states to consider. States could tailor any portion of the laws to meet their specific needs and pass state legislation accordingly.

Although the Model State Drug Laws focused on helping states curb the abuse of alcohol and illegal drugs, the problem of prescription drug abuse did not go unnoticed. Therefore, the commission also drafted the Model Prescription Accountability Act, designed to stop diversion of pharmaceuticals without impeding legitimate prescribing. "If done properly, monitoring programs create a number of opportunities to prevent drug abuse, addiction, and the suffering before it happens," says Sherry Green, Executive Director of the National Alliance for Model State Drug Laws. "So many laws are set up to deal with the aftereffects of a problem, but this is a chance to be proactive."

At the heart of the Model Prescription Accountability Act was the recommendation for electronic monitoring systems that would collect information on doctors, pharmacists, and patients receiving controlled substances, and compare it with programmed criteria to detect suspicious prescriptions. The act provided a foundation for states to build upon in their efforts to combat prescription drug abuse and its damaging personal and societal effects. Monitoring programs can help in the following ways:

- Drug abusers are deterred from acquiring drugs to self-medicate.
- Those obtaining fraudulent prescriptions can be confronted and referred to treatment.
- Physicians and pharmacists can help stop abuse by identifying doctor shoppers and pharmacy shoppers.
- Law enforcement agencies can detect diversion more quickly.
- States can determine how serious the legal drug problem is and consider education programs, laws, and policies accordingly.

To learn whether your state has a prescription drug monitoring program, visit the Web site of the National Alliance for Model State Drug Laws at www.namsdl.org.

How Do Prescription Drug Monitoring Systems Work?

Basically, after a customer takes a prescription to a pharmacy, the pharmacy sends computerized information to the state agency's confidential prescription drug database. Typically, the information submitted includes the name of the prescriber, his or her DEA number, the pharmacy's identification number, the patient's name or identification number (often the driver's license number), and the National Drug Code, which tells the strength and form of the drug. The data also include the quantity of the drug dispensed and date the prescription was filled.

There are two types of monitoring programs—reactive and proactive. The *reactive programs* provide reports about a patient's past prescriptions only when a report is requested by a prescribing doctor, pharmacist, or authorized law enforcement agent; any of these individuals can log in to the state's database to see if an individual has been obtaining multiple prescriptions. Health professionals can better determine whether a patient is seeking legitimate medical help or if the patient is diverting drugs to support an addiction, and law enforcement can investigate individuals seeking to acquire suspicious prescriptions.

The *proactive programs* are set up to generate unsolicited reports on individuals who appear to be acquiring controlled substances in a suspicious manner. From these reports, suspicious individuals can be identified and investigated. States with proactive programs are more law enforcement oriented in their approach.

Monitoring Drugs according to Schedule

States with prescription monitoring programs choose which "schedules" of drugs they will monitor. Controlled substances are ranked by schedules, or categories. The schedule into which a drug is placed depends on these factors:

- Known potential for physical or psychological harm
- Potential for abuse
- Accepted medical use
- Accepted safety under medical supervision

How were the schedules established? Recognizing the abuse potential of many medications, Congress enacted the Controlled Substances Act of 1970 to better regulate the manufacture, distribution, and dispensation of controlled substances. The legislation called for dividing controlled substances into five schedules. For example, Schedule I drugs include such illegal substances as heroin and cocaine. They have a high potential for abuse, but no generally accepted medical use in the United States, and are not available through legal means. Schedules II through V contain drugs with accepted medical uses and abuse potential. Schedule II pharmaceuticals are the most likely to be abused; Schedule V drugs are the least likely to be abused. (See Appendix A in the back of the book for a listing of controlled substances by schedule.)

State Prescription Drug Monitoring Programs

The following information is a sampling of the prescription drug monitoring programs some states have set up to help combat the diversion of drugs from health-care professionals.

Oklahoma

The Oklahoma Prescription Monitoring Program was one of the first electronic monitoring programs in the nation. It went online in January 1991, and originally the program monitored only Schedule II drugs; however, in 2006, Schedule III, IV, and V drugs were added.

The Oklahoma program is set up so that prescribing doctors, pharmacists, and law enforcement officials can request information about a patient whom they believe may be trying to acquire prescription drugs suspiciously. "Ninety-three percent of the requests for reports on a patient come from physicians," says Don Vogt, manager of the Oklahoma program. "The monitoring program is helpful in stopping doctor shopping. We discovered one man who was getting narcotics from sixty-six doctors. We also had one doctor's clinic that was able to identify sixty-two patients who were getting drugs from multiple doctors. Before 2006, we were seeing as many as 120 classic doctor shoppers monthly. Now that number has dropped to 20 or 30 per month."

The Oklahoma monitoring program can also examine the prescribing practices of doctors; however, the state has had few problems with inappropriate prescribing, according to Vogt. "We have about 14,000 doctors in the state, and only in rare cases have we investigated a doctor; I would say we have investigated less than 1 percent of our doctors for suspicious prescribing."

The annual operating costs of the Oklahoma monitoring program are approximately $350,000.

Kentucky

The state of Kentucky's monitoring program is known as KASPER, which stands for Kentucky All Schedule Prescription Electronic Reporting. It went into effect in 1999 and keeps track of drugs prescribed in Schedules II through V. The program offers a Web-based program so that doctors, pharmacists, and law enforcement officials can request a report and receive it in fifteen to twenty seconds.

When prescription monitoring programs were first adopted, many physicians opposed them, believing that such oversight by the state government would interfere with their ability to prescribe medications, especially painkillers, to patients who legitimately needed them. However, statistics gathered by the state show that doctors' prescribing patterns have not changed and that most doctors have embraced the system.

According to Dave Hopkins, manager of the Kentucky monitoring program, "In 2000, we had 36,172 requests for reports from doctors. In 2007, we had 361,658 requests for such reports. That's nearly a 1,000 percent increase. And doctors make up the biggest group, 93 percent, of those requesting reports."

Additional statistics show that 92 percent of doctors are satisfied with the program, and 95 percent of them view KASPER as an effective way to identify potential doctor shoppers. Further, many doctors report that they are more comfortable now in prescribing narcotics. The annual operating costs of the program are $350,000.

Nevada

The state of Nevada went online with its electronic prescription monitoring program in January 1997. It monitors all Schedule II, III, and IV controlled substance prescriptions. The PMP permits physicians and pharmacists to retrieve "patient profiles" from the state's database, allowing them to determine what other drugs their patients might be obtaining. This action helps health professionals from becoming victims of doctor shoppers. It also helps doctors and pharmacists refer chemically dependent patients to treatment rather than having them prosecuted and sent to jail.

A review of the program's history shows that it was effective early on. Almost immediately after the Nevada program began, it thwarted doctor shoppers. During the first year, profiles were developed for 182 individuals, all probable doctor shoppers. Profile results showed each had obtained an average of 159 prescriptions for controlled substances from twenty-two different physicians and had gotten them filled at sixteen different pharmacies. The first major doctor shopper case detected by the Nevada monitoring program involved a man who visited eighty doctors in a twelve-month period; he had 216 prescriptions for controlled substances, which he had filled at eighty-four pharmacies.

Since the program's inception, more and more health professionals have taken advantage of the "two-way" reporting system and have increasingly asked for more profiles on patients they suspect of abusing drugs. Annual operating costs are $300,000.

California

In 2008, California took steps to launch the Controlled Substance Utilization Review and Evaluation system, a prescription drug monitoring program, the largest online patient database in the nation. Once completed, it will allow doctors and pharmacists to go into the database to check a patient's prescription history—all in an effort to thwart doctor shopping and other efforts to obtain prescription drugs fraudulently.

In the past, the California attorney general's office has received 60,000 requests annually from doctors and pharmacists, seeking information about patient prescription histories. These requests were sent by fax or telephone, and processing them took days. The new system allows health-care professionals to check a patient's prescription history within a few seconds.

Part of the driving force behind the monitoring program came from Bob and Carmen Pack, a California couple who worked to raise $3.5 million dollars needed to start the monitoring system. The Packs' two children, Troy, ten, and Alana, seven, were killed in 2003 when a drugged driver's car jumped the curb and hit them as they walked down the sidewalk. The woman driving the car was under the influence of six prescription drugs, obtained from multiple doctors. (She was sentenced to thirty years in prison for second-degree murder.)

New York

In 1972, the state of New York first started monitoring the prescription drugs Xanax and Valium. They have continually upgraded their program and, in 2000, started monitoring drugs in schedules II through V. The New York program collects data and sends reports to health professionals once a month; these reports contain the names of people who are seeing multiple physicians within a thirty-day period. "We do not follow up with these doctors; instead, we encourage them to refer the patients to addiction treatment or to pain management experts," states James Giglio, Director of the New York Bureau of Narcotic Enforcement.

In 2007, the program identified 740 individuals who visited eight or nine doctors during one month's time. These patients saw a total of 4,500 doctors and generated 11,000 prescriptions.

New York's program is unique in that it furnishes all health professionals with prescription pads that have high-tech security features, making it virtually impossible to make counterfeit copies. The pads contain the names of doctors, and each page of the pad has a serial number. Doctors are required to report any missing or stolen pads. The annual operating costs for the New York program are $17 million; much of this amount goes toward the production of the specialized prescription pads.

Monitoring Does Not Affect Doctors' Prescribing

When monitoring programs first came about, many physicians expressed concerns that such scrutiny might impair them from prescribing drugs, especially pain medications, for patients who legitimately needed them. However, as the programs have evolved, such opposition has dissipated. Doctors have learned that the monitoring programs help them identify doctor shoppers, and the programs have not had a "chilling effect" on prescribing practices.

A look at the New York program's statistics shows that doctors have not cut back on legitimate prescribing of pain medications. For example, from 2003 to 2006, New York health professionals prescribed nearly 2 million painkillers. In 2006, they prescribed 4.5 million painkillers—that is a 115 percent increase. "We have worked diligently to convince doctors that we are not the enemy," says Giglio. "We are here to assist them and the public in an effort to curtail the diversion of drugs."

11

Law Enforcement Efforts

Is doctor shopping against the law? Is forging prescriptions illegal? Yes, both are illegal, and in many states they are felonies. Do law enforcement agencies pursue such crimes? In some cases, yes. In other cases, no—most cities are understaffed and underfunded when it comes to investigating prescription drug diversion.

Historically, law enforcement's attitude about prescription drug abuse has reflected that of society as a whole—it has not been viewed as a serious problem. Accordingly, for decades most of the training and resources for law enforcement agencies have focused on illicit drugs. John Burke, President of the National Association of Drug Diversion Investigators, sums it up this way: "Doctors and pharmacists have known this prescription problem has existed for years, but often they've not had law enforcement to turn to in the community. If law enforcement is not working on the problem, whom do the health professionals call?"

Still, in recent years, some law enforcement agencies have taken a more-active role in the investigation of prescription fraud and have made strides in combating the problem.

Local Efforts

Compared to many other cities, Louisville, Kentucky, population 1 million, is one city that has been comparatively proactive in investigating prescription drug diversion. Between 2006 and 2007, the city's Metro Narcotics Unit had four detectives and a sergeant. During that two-year period, they arrested 414 individuals, who collectively had acquired nearly 139,000 pills through illegal means.

"We get calls from doctors and pharmacists, reporting suspicious individuals," says Stan Salyards, sergeant for the narcotics unit. "We have spent years developing a close working relationship with the city's doctors and pharmacists. They know they can call us twenty-four hours a day, and we'll respond. We also have a fax number, dedicated to receiving complaints about doctor shoppers and others who are trying to acquire drugs illegally. Those faxes come in daily."

One of the facts to be realized from the Louisville example is that these types of prescription drug–related crimes are occurring in cities across the nation; and many of these cities have even fewer law enforcement resources than Louisville has to combat the problem.

Some cities in Ohio have also been more proactive in combating prescription drug diversion. Dale Smith is a drug diversion detective in Westshore, about fifteen miles outside Cleveland. His jurisdiction has a population of 200,000. "Doctor shopping and forging or altering prescriptions are the main ways I've seen people obtaining drugs illegally," says Smith. "Two years ago, we arrested a young man who had visited 101 doctors and about fifty pharmacies to acquire Vicodin; he was taking nearly fifty tablets a day. His case was extreme." In 2007, Smith investigated a total of 104 individuals for prescription drug diversion. He also reports that the state's prescription drug monitoring program is beginning to be helpful, too.

Factors Influencing Prescription Drug Diversion

- *Drug abusers are more sophisticated.* They learn how to produce certain psychological effects with combinations of pharmaceuticals that are more predictable in terms of purity, onset, and duration of effect. This means less chance of overdosing.
- *Less risk of detection and arrest.* In some areas, defrauding physicians or pharmacists is only a misdemeanor, in contrast to the felony offense for dealing illicit drugs. Pharmaceuticals are also often easier to obtain.
- *Financial gain.* Prescription drugs are usually not as expensive as illicit drugs. If purchased at retail prices, the sale of pharmaceuticals can be lucrative. For example, the painkiller Dilaudid may cost $2 per tablet when purchased in a drugstore, but may be sold on the street for $50 to $100 per tablet.
- *Urine testing by employers.* Often, if a job candidate can demonstrate that he or she is taking a prescription drug and even show the prescription bottle, the candidate is often exempt from negative consequences if a urine test is positive. Sometimes, having a prescription bottle handy will preclude having a urine test altogether.
- *Less risk of disease, especially AIDS.* As addicts look for ways to minimize their risk of HIV infection, more users are turning to prescription drugs because the product is pure, and an oral form can be used rather than an intravenous one. A prime example is the use of Dilaudid instead of injected heroin.

State Efforts

At the state level, investigations of drug diversion may be carried out by state law enforcement agencies and/or members of health regulatory boards, including those for pharmacists, nurses, and physicians. Since members of regulatory boards lack the authority to make arrests, they will usually turn matters over to law enforcement agencies after completing an investigation.

Still, most law enforcement agencies have limited funding to hire the investigators and other staff needed to combat the problem. Some states may have only one or two investigators.

Virginia was one of the first states to allocate resources to investigate prescription drug diversion. Its Drug Diversion Unit, part of the Virginia State Police, is one of the largest state-level investigative units, with seventeen investigators. The diversion unit investigates two basic categories of individuals. One group includes the doctor shoppers and prescription forgers; these individuals may be acquiring the drugs to self-medicate or sell, or both. The second group includes health professionals—doctors, nurses, and pharmacists who are found to be self-medicating.

Investigating Doctor Shoppers

How is a typical doctor-shopping case handled in Virginia? The diversion investigative unit may get a complaint about someone suspected of doctor shopping; the call may come from a doctor, a pharmacist, a family member, or a friend. If an agent is assigned, he or she interviews the doctors and pharmacists involved, and attempts to find out whether the individual is seeing more than one doctor to obtain similar drugs. If the agent determines that one of the doctors would not have prescribed a drug had he or she known the patient was getting the drug from another source, the violation of law is established. One doctor shopper is arrested every nine days in Virginia. One prescription forger is arrested every ten days.

Investigating Drug Sellers

There are certainly more individuals who doctor shop to obtain drugs for themselves than those who acquire the drugs to resell them; however, arresting a dealer can have more impact than the arrest of a single doctor shopper. The Virginia unit also keeps a focus on drug sellers. In one investigation, they uncovered a ring of scammers in Virginia, Maryland, and Washington, D.C., who were able to divert Dilaudid, a painkiller, by printing their own prescription pads. They used various doctors' names and their DEA numbers when writing the prescriptions. The scammers even had bogus phone numbers for doctors' offices—a bank of pay phones they'd set up. Ring members would identify themselves as employees of one of the doctors when a pharmacist would call to verify a prescription. All were eventually arrested.

Investigating Health Professionals

It's believed that the rate of addiction among health professionals may be slightly higher than that of the general population due to their access to controlled substances and the stresses of their work. The statistics on arrests of health professionals in Virginia reflects this belief. In Virginia, one doctor is investigated every ten days, and one doctor is arrested every thirty-five days. Among all health-care professionals in the state, one is arrested every six days.

Community Education

Part of the success of the Virginia program is a result of the community education programs provided by the Virginia diversion investigative unit. They provide continuing education to health professionals—hospital employees and administrators, doctors, nurses, and pharmacists. Seminars cover such topics as how to spot scammers, drugs of abuse, and laws against diversion.

International Smuggling

In 2004, investigators in Ohio disrupted an international smuggling operation. State investigators were finding numerous people in the area in possession of what turned out to be illegal versions of the tranquilizer Xanax. In the course of the investigation, they discovered that the pills were Upjohn 90s, a generic form of the drug; however, the drugs were for distribution only in Mexico and South America. The drugs were being smuggled into the United States and sold on the black market.

John Burke, of the National Association of Drug Diversion Investigators, was involved with the investigation. "We arrested the guy who was bringing the drugs into Ohio. He was going to San Antonio twice a month and buying 100,000 of these Xanax. He'd pay 50 cents apiece and then sell them in the United States for a dollar each. He was making $50,000 with each trip he made."

It turns out this activity was also occurring in other parts of the United States, according to Burke. "I thought the case was closed, but about a year later, I was in Tennessee for an addiction seminar. A local police officer stood up and asked if any investigators in the room had come across Upjohn 90s that were being smuggled into the country. So this smuggling operation was occurring in other states, as well."

Federal Efforts

In recent years, federal efforts in the "war against drugs" have been expanded to include the diversion of prescription drugs. The White House Office on National Drug Control Policy advocates an approach that includes prevention, education, and treatment. Federal efforts, including congressional action, also include a crackdown on illegal Internet pharmacies.

Some successes have been reported. For example, in August 2007, a business called Affpower was discovered to have grossed $126 million dollars in the illegal sale of prescription drugs. The company was indicted on 313 counts, as were eighteen individuals. During the same period, the owner of Express Pharmacy Direct was sentenced to thirty years in federal prison for operating an illegal online pharmacy that sold controlled substances to individuals who did not have legitimate prescriptions.

Drug Enforcement Administration Efforts

The mission of the Drug Enforcement Administration (DEA) is to enforce the controlled-substances laws and regulations of the United States. Part of the DEA mandate is to control pharmaceutical diversion. The DEA is not actually a law enforcement agency; however, it employs field investigators who typically team with other investigators, including those from the FBI, U.S. Customs, FDA, and state and local authorities. The DEA puts its focus on the "bigger players" who may be diverting larger amounts of controlled substances, rather than on the single doctor shopper who acquires drugs for his or her own use.

The DEA estimates that the black market, or illegal diversion of controlled substances, constitutes a multibillion-dollar annual market. For example, an OxyContin tablet prescribed for pain is a sought-after drug on the street. In pharmacies, the drug may cost the consumer $4 per tablet, but on the street it may sell for $10 to $40 or more per tablet. A cancer patient might commonly receive a prescription of 200 to 300 tablets with a street value upwards of $12,000.

In one case, DEA agents arrested a physician in Chicago who was obtaining pain relievers and tranquilizers and taking them to Las Vegas, where he sold them, in bags of thirty tablets, in a vitamin store. At the time of his arrest at a Chicago airport, he had 30,000 hydrocodone tablets in his suitcases. Investigators later determined that the doctor had diverted more than 500,000 tablets of hydrocodone and other controlled substances. He was convicted and sentenced to four years in prison.

Tactical Diversion Squads

In the late 1990s, the DEA established *tactical diversion squads* to investigate prescription drug diversion. Federally funded, these groups are comprised of DEA investigators and state and local law enforcement officers. The squads are assigned to investigate local diversions.

Tracking Shipments of Narcotics

Prescription drug diversion has no geographical boundaries—it occurs throughout the United States. To help track the shipping of controlled substances, the DEA uses an automated system known as ARCOS—Automation of Reports and Consolidated Orders System. This system keeps track of where drugs are being shipped, from the point of manufacture to the point of sale.

In recent years, the DEA has also begun making use of prescription data collected by IMS Health, a private company that tracks pharmaceuticals sales and dispensation across the nation. Armed with IMS data, the DEA observes patterns in prescriptions being filled according to zip code.

In Closing

Never doubt the power of small groups to change the world; indeed, it is the only thing that ever has.

—Margaret Mead, anthropologist
1901–1978

The country's addiction problems with all substances—alcohol, tobacco, illegal drugs, and legal drugs—represent one of our nation's most serious health hazards. Not only does addiction shred the emotional fabric of our families, but the consequences of untreated substance abuse include premature deaths, traffic accidents, poor health, AIDS, dropping out of school, joblessness, underemployment, worker absenteeism, and reduced worker productivity.

More than half a million people die every year because of substance abuse. Long-term drug abuse can reduce life expectancy by about fifteen years. About 50 percent of all preventable deaths are related to some aspect of substance abuse. One out of every five hospital beds is occupied by a person with substance abuse as a contributing factor.

Historically, as a nation, we have taken prescription drug abuse too lightly as a health issue. We need much greater public awareness about this hidden epidemic.

How do we fix this problem? There is no simple answer. The problem is a multifaceted one. But, clearly, education is key. Among the things we can do to combat prescription drug addiction:

- Increase consumer education about addiction and drugs of addiction
- Increase continuing education on addiction for health professionals
- Make addiction treatment programs more accessible
- Promote prevention programs in schools and for the public
- Fund law enforcement resources for drug diversion investigation
- Shut down the illegal Internet pharmacies
- Implement treatment programs as part of the justice system for offenders
- Implement prescription monitoring programs

We can readily see that some of the measures that have already been instituted, such as addiction treatment programs and state monitoring programs, *do* produce positive results. We can expand these types of efforts. As a society, we have the intelligence and the ability to make these changes. Now, we must strengthen our resolve to make the changes. Only then can we eliminate the suffering caused by drug abuse and save more lives.

Appendix A

Categories of Controlled Substances

The drugs listed below are those that are commonly abused. For a full list of drugs in each of the schedule categories, go to the Drug Enforcement Administration Web site at www.deadiversion.usdoj.gov/schedules.

Schedule I

These illegal drugs have no legitimate medical use.

- Heroin
- Marijuana
- MDMA (ecstasy)
- Methaqualone (quaalude)
- Phencyclidine (PCP)
- LSD
- MDA
- Mescaline
- Peyote
- Psilocybin

Schedule II

High potential for abuse. Use may lead to severe physical or psychological dependence. Prescriptions must be written in ink or typewritten and signed by the practitioner. Verbal prescriptions must be confirmed in writing within seventy-two hours and may be given only in a genuine emergency. No refills are permitted.

- Alfentanil *(Alfenta)*
- Amobarbital *(Amytal)*
- Amphetamine *(Dexedrine, Adderall)*
- Cocaine
- Codeine
- Fentanyl *(Sublimaze, Duragesic)*
- Glutethimide
- Hydromorphone *(Dilaudid)*
- Levomethadyl *(LAAM)*
- Levorphanol *(Levo-Dromoran)*
- Meperidine *(Demerol)*
- Methadone *(Dolophine)*
- Methamphetamine (*Desoxyn*)
- Methylphenidate *(Ritalin)*
- Morphine (*MS Contin, Oramorph, Roxanol, Duramorph,* others)
- Opium
- Oxycodone *(OxyContin, Percodan, Percocet, Roxicodone, Tylox)*
- Oxymorphone *(Numorphan)*
- Pentobarbital *(Nembutal)*
- Phenmetrazine *(Preludin)*
- Secobarbital *(Seconal)*
- Sufentanil *(Sufenta)*

Schedule III

Potential for abuse. Use may lead to low-to-moderate physical dependence or high psychological dependence. Prescriptions may be oral or written. Up to five refills are permitted within six months.

- Anabolic steroids (*Anadrol-50, Deca-Durabolin, Halotestin, Oxandrin, Winstrol)*
- Benzphetamine *(Didrex)*

- Buprenorphine *(Buprenex, Subutex)*
- Butabarbital *(Butisol)*
- Butalbital (*Fiorinal, Fioricet*)
- Camphorated tincture of opium (paregoric)
- Codeine (low doses combined with non-narcotic medications such as acetaminophen *[Tylenol with Codeine* or aspirin, *Empirin with Codeine* or *Soma Compound with Codeine]*)
- Dronabinol *(Marinol)*
- Hydrocodone (with acetaminophen—*Lorcet, Lortab, Vicodin;* with aspirin—*Lortab ASA;* with chlorpheniramine—*Tussionex*)
- Nalorphine (*Nalline)*
- Phendimetrazine *(Prelu-2)*
- Testosterone

Schedule IV

Potential for abuse. Use may lead to physical or psychological dependence. Prescriptions may be oral or written. Up to five refills are permitted within six months.

- Alprazolam *(Xanax)*
- Butorphanol (*Stadol*)
- Chloral Hydrate (*Noctec*)
- Chlordiazepoxide *(Librium, Libritabs)*
- Clonazepam *(Klonopin)*
- Clorazepate *(Tranxene)*
- Diazepam *(Valium)*
- Flurazepam *(Dalmane)*
- Lorazepam *(Ativan)*
- Mephobarbital *(Mebaral)*
- Meprobamate *(Equanil, Miltown)*
- Midazolam *(Versed*)
- Oxazepam *(Serax)*
- Pemoline (*Cylert*)

- Pentazocine *(Talwin)*
- Phentermine *(Fastin)*
- Phenobarbital (*Luminal*)
- Propoxyphene *(Darvon, Darvocet)*
- Quazepam *(Doral)*
- Temazepam (*Restoril*)
- Triazolam *(Halcion)*

Schedule V

Subject to state and local regulation. Abuse potential is low; addictive medication is often combined with nonaddicting medicines to reduce abuse potential. A prescription may not be required.

- Codeine (in low doses combined with non-narcotic medication—*Tussi-Organidin)*
- Diphenoxylate *(Lomotil)*

Appendix B

Drugs to Avoid If You're over Sixty-Five

Tranquilizers, Sleeping Aids

- Chlordiazepoxide *(Librium, Mitran)* tranquilizer. Causes falls.
- Diazepam *(Valium)* tranquilizer. Addictive, too long-acting.
- Flurazepam *(Dalmane)* sleeping aid. May cause falls.
- Meprobamate (*Miltown, Equagesic, Equanil)* tranquilizer. May cause falls.
- Pentobarbital *(Nembutal)* sedative. Addictive.
- Quazepam *(Doral)* May cause drowsiness, dizziness, lightheadedness, or difficulty with coordination. Addictive.
- Secobarbital *(Seconal)* sedative. Addictive.
- Temazepam *(Restoril)* Anxiety; clumsiness or unsteadiness; daytime drowsiness; dizziness; fatigue; feeling of hangover; headache; lightheadedness; nausea; nervousness; sluggishness; unusual weakness. Addictive.
- Triazolam *(Halcion)* May cause drowsiness, dizziness, lightheadedness, or difficulty with coordination.

Antidepressants

- Amitriptyline *(Elavil)* Often causes inability to urinate, dizziness, and drowsiness.
- Chlordiazepoxide-amitriptyline *(Limbitrol)* Blurred vision, dizziness, headache, and nausea are common side effects.
- Doxepin *(Sinequan)* May cause drowsiness, dizziness, or blurred vision. The elderly may be more sensitive to its effects.
- Fluoxetine *(Prozac)* The elderly should use with caution as they may be more sensitive to its effects, especially low blood sodium levels.

Arthritis Drugs

- Indomethacin *(Indocin, Indocin SR)* Causes confusion, headaches.
- Naproxen *(Naprosyn, Avaprox, Aleve)* May cause an increased risk of serious and sometimes fatal stomach ulcers and bleeding.
- Oxaprozin *(Daypro)* May cause dizziness or drowsiness. The elderly may be more sensitive to its effects, including stomach bleeding and kidney problems.
- Piroxicam *(Feldene)* May cause dizziness or drowsiness. The elderly may be more sensitive to its effects, including stomach bleeding and kidney problems.

Diabetes Drugs

- Chlorpropamide *(Diabinese)* Can cause dangerous fluid retention.

Pain Relievers

- Ketorolac *(Toradol)* The elderly may be more sensitive to the effects. Dizziness, drowsiness, and headache are common side effects.

- Meperidine *(Demerol)* Addictive. More-common side effects may include: dizziness, light-headedness, and sedation.
- Pentazocine *(Talwin)* Addictive.
- Propoxyphene *(Darvon, Darvocet)* Addictive and little more effective than aspirin.

Dementia Treatments

- Ergot mesyloids *(Hydergine)* Stomach upset, temporary nausea.
- Isoxsuprine *(Vasodilan)* Not shown to be effective.

Blood Thinners

- Dipyridamole *(Persantine)* Except for patients with artificial heart valves, not shown to be effective.
- Ticlopidine *(Ticlid)* Common side effects are: diarrhea, indigestion, nausea, stomach pain, and vomiting.

Muscle Relaxants, Spasm Relievers

- Carisoprodol *(Soma)* Potential for central nervous system toxicity.
- Chlorzoxazone *(Paraflex)* May cause drowsiness, dizziness, or restlessness.
- Cyclobenzaprine *(Flexeril)* Can cause dizziness, drowsiness, fainting.
- Metaxalone *(Skelaxin)* Common side effects are: dizziness, drowsiness, headache, and nervousness.
- Methocarbamol *(Robaxin)* May cause dizziness or drowsiness.
- Orphenadrine *(Norflex, Norgesic)* Can cause dizziness, drowsiness, fainting.

Antihypertensive Drugs

- Clonidine *(Catapres)* Dizziness, drowsiness, tiredness, and nausea are common side effects.
- Doxazosin *(Cardura)* May cause dizziness or drowsiness.
- Guanadrel *(Hylorel)* May cause unusual fatigue, drowsiness, or dizziness.
- Propranolol *(Inderal)* Feeling slowed mentally and physically.
- Reserpine *(Serpalan, Serpasil)* Depression.

Antianxiety Drugs

- Alpraxolam *(Xanax)* May cause dizziness or fainting. Addictive.
- lorazepate *(Tranxene)* Elderly in weakened condition are more apt to become unsteady or oversedated.
- Hydroxyzine *(Vistaril, Atarax)* Drowsiness. The elderly may be more sensitive to its effects.
- Lorazepam *(Ativan)* Clumsiness, dizziness, drowsiness, and unsteadiness are common side effects. The elderly may be more sensitive to its effects.
- Oxazepam *(Serax)* The elderly may be more sensitive to its effects, especially lightheadedness, particularly when standing.

Heart Medications

- Amiodarone *(Cordarone, Pacerone)* May cause dizziness, fatigue, lack of coordination.
- Digoxin *(Lanoxin)* May cause dizziness or blurred vision.
- Disopyramide *(Norpace, Norpace CR)* May cause blurred vision and dizziness.
- Ethacrynic acid *(Edecrin)* May cause dizziness, lightheadedness, or fainting. The elderly may be more sensitive to its effects.

- Nifedipine *(Procardia, Adalat)* Side effects may include: dizziness, fatigue, giddiness, lightheadedness, and mood changes.

Attention-Deficit Hyperactivity Disorder (ADHD) Drugs

- Amphetamines *(Adderall)* May cause high blood pressure, dizziness, and weight loss.

Stomach and Intestinal Medications

- Belladonna alkaloids *(Donnatal, Hyosophen)* May cause blurred vision, clumsiness, dizziness, lightheadedness.
- Bisacodyl *(Dulcolax)* May cause faintness, cramps, or stomach discomfort.
- Cascara segrada (generic) Stomach upset, rectal bleeding, stomach pain or cramps.
- Cimetidine *(Tagamet)* Common side effects are: diarrhea, dizziness, drowsiness, and headache.
- Clidinium-chlordizaepoxide *(Librax)* Blurred vision, clumsiness, confusion, and dizziness are common side effects.
- Dicyclomine *(Bentyl)* May cause drowsiness, dizziness, blurred vision, or lightheadedness. The elderly may be more sensitive to its effects.
- Hyoscyamine *(Levsin, Levsinex)* The elderly may be more sensitive to its effects, especially constipation, trouble urinating, drowsiness, agitation, confusion, or excitement.
- Propantheline *(Pro-Banthine)* May cause drowsiness, dizziness, blurred vision, or lightheadedness.

Respiratory Tract and Sinus Medications

- Chlorpheniramine *(Chlor-Trimeton, Ahist)* Dizziness, drowsiness, headache, loss of appetite are common side effects.
- Cyproheptadine *(Periactin)* Can cause sleepiness, fatigue, or dizziness.
- Dexchlorpheniramine *(Polaramine)* Common side effects are sleepiness, fatigue, or dizziness.
- Diphenhydramine *(Benadryl)* Can cause sleepiness, fatigue, or dizziness. Patients over sixty years of age may be more likely to experience side effects and may require a lower dose of this medication.
- Promethazine *(Phenergan)* May cause drowsiness or dizziness. The elderly may be more sensitive to its effects.

Schizophrenia Drugs

- Thioridazine *(Mellaril)* Mild restlessness, drowsiness, or tremor.

Hypogonadism Drugs

- Methyltestosterone *(Android, Virilon, Testrad)* The elderly may be more sensitive to its effects, especially enlarged prostate and prostate cancer.

Urinary Tract Drugs

- Nitrofurantoin *(Macrodantin)* Can cause shortness of breath, fever, chest pains, numbness, or tingling.
- Oxybutynin *(Ditropan)* May cause drowsiness, dizziness, or blurred vision.

From a summary of information from the following report in *Archives of Internal Medicine*. Source: Fick, D.M., Cooper, J.W., Wade, W.E., Walter, J.L., Maclean, J.R., Beers, M.H. Updating the Beers criteria for potentially inappropriate medication use in older adults: results of a US consensus panel of experts. *Arch Intern Med.* 2003;163:2716-2724.

Resources

American Association for the Treatment of Opioid Dependence, Inc. (Methadone)

255 Varick Street, 4th Floor
New York, NY 10014
(212) 566-5555
www.aatod.org

American Chronic Pain Association

P.O. Box 850
Rocklin, CA 95677
(800) 533-3231
www.theacpa.org

American Pain Foundation

201 North Charles Street, Suite 710
Baltimore, MD 21201-4111
(888) 615-7246
www.painfoundation.org

American Pain Society

4700 West Lake Avenue
Glenview, IL 60025
(847) 375-4715
www.ampainsoc.org

American Pharmacists Association (APhA)

1100 15th Street NW, Suite 400
Washington, DC 20005
(202) 628-4410
www.aphanet.org

American Psychiatric Association
1000 Wilson Boulevard, Suite 1825
Arlington, VA 22209
1-888-357-7924
www.apa@psych.org

American Society of Addiction Medicine (ASAM)
4601 North Park Avenue, Arcade Suite 101
Chevy Chase, MD 20815
(301) 656-3920
www.asam.org

Buprenorphine (Suboxone) Treatment Peer-Support
P.O. Box 333
Farmington, CT 06034
(860) 269-4390
www.naabt.org

Community Anti-Drug Coalitions of America (CADCA)
625 Slaters Lane, Suite 300
Alexandria, VA 22314
1-800-54-CADCA
www.cadca.org

Faces and Voices of Recovery
1010 Vermont Avenue, Room 708
Washington, DC 20005
(202) 737-0690
www.facesandvoicesofrecovery.org

Nar-Anon Family Group Headquarters
22527 Crenshaw Boulevard, No. 200B
Torrance, CA 90505
(310) 534-8188
www.nar-anon.org

Narcotics Anonymous (NA)
World Service Office in Los Angeles
P.O. Box 9999
Van Nuys, CA 91409
(818) 700-9999
www.na.org

National Alliance for Model State Drug Laws
700 North Fairfax Street, Suite 306
Alexandria, VA 22314

703-836-6100
www.namsdl.org

National Alliance of Methadone Advocates
435 Second Avenue
New York, NY 10010
212-595-6262
www.methadone.org

National Association of Addiction Treatment Providers (NAATP)
313 West Liberty Street, Suite 129
Lancaster, PA 17603
(717) 392-8480
www.naatp.org

National Association of Chain Drug Stores
413 North Lee Street
Alexandria, VA 22313
(703) 549-3001
www.nacds.org

National Association of Drug Court Professionals
4900 Seminary Road, Suite 320
Alexandria, VA 22311
(703) 575-9400
www.nadcp.org

National Association of Drug Diversion Investigators (NADDI)
P.O. Box 611
Manchester, MD 21102
(443) 398-6257
www.naddi.org

National Association of State Controlled Substance Authorities (NASCSA)
72 Brook Street
Quincy, MA 02170
(617) 472-0520
www.nascsa.org

National Center on Addiction and Substance Abuse (CASA)
633 Third Avenue, 19th Floor
New York, NY 10017-6706
(212) 841-5200
www.casacolumbia.org

National Council on Patient Information and Education (NCPIE)
4915 St. Elmo Avenue, Suite 505
Bethesda, MD 20814
(301) 656-8565
www.talkaboutrx.org

National Institute on Drug Abuse (NIDA)
6001 Executive Boulevard, Room 5213
Bethesda, MD 20892
(301) 443-1124
www.nida.nih.gov

Office of National Drug Control Policy
P.O. Box 6000
Rockville, MD 20849
(800) 666-3332
www.whitehousedrugpolicy.gov

Partnership for a Drug-Free America
405 Lexington Avenue, Suite 1601
New York, NY 10174
(212) 922-1560
www.drugfree.org

Pharmaceutical Research and Manufacturers of America (PhRMA)
950 F Street NW
Washington, DC 20004
(202) 835-3400
www.phrma.org

Substance Abuse and Mental Health Services Administration (SAMHSA)
5600 Fishers Lane
Rockville, MD 20857
(301) 443-5052
www.samhsa.gov

SAMHSA Substance Abuse Treatment Facility Locator
www.findtreatment.samhsa.gov

This searchable directory lists locations of facilities around the country that treat alcohol and drug abuse problems. The locator includes more than 12,000 residential treatment centers, inpatient treatment programs, and outpatient treatment programs for drug abuse and addiction and alcoholism.

U.S. Drug Enforcement Administration (DEA)
Office of Diversion Control
Attn: Liaison and Policy Section
Washington, DC 20537
www.deadiversion.usdoj.gov

Index

About the Author

After my brother died, I wanted to help others who are devastated by prescription drug addiction. It's a perplexing problem, and life doesn't come with a training manual on what to do when you or a loved one becomes addicted. I hope this book will provide some measure of insight and comfort.

Rod Colvin describes his passion for the topic of prescription drug addiction as coming from the death of his brother Randy, who died at age thirty-five, as a result of his long-term addiction to prescription drugs. *Overcoming Prescription Drug Addiction* is the third edition of this book, previously published as *Prescription Drug Addiction—The Hidden Epidemic* (2001).

In 2005, Colvin served on an advisory panel for the National Center on Addiction and Substance Abuse (CASA), which conducted the nation's first landmark study on prescription drug abuse in America. The study, *Under the Counter: The Diversion and Abuse of Prescription Drugs in the United States*, was published in July 2005. Downloadable copies are available at www.casacolumbia.org.

Colvin is the publisher of Addicus Books, Inc., which he founded in 1994. Based in Omaha, Nebraska, the company's focus is consumer health books. Colvin is a former member of the board of directors of the Independent Book Publisher's Association, a trade association consisting of 4,000 independent publishers across the United States.

Colvin is the author of two other nonfiction books, *Evil Harvest* (Bantam Books, 1992) and *First Heroes* (Irvington Publishers, 1987); a former broadcast journalist, he has also written and produced radio and television documentaries.

He holds a bachelor of arts degree in sociology from Washburn University, Topeka, Kansas, and a master of science degree in counseling psychology from Emporia State University, Emporia, Kansas.

Rod Colvin may be reached through his Web site:

www.prescriptiondrugaddiction.com

Book Order Form

Please send:

________copies of ____

at__________each.

Total ____________________

Nebraska residents add 6.5% sales tax ____________________

Shipping/Handling ____________________

$4.60 postage for first book: ____________________

$1.10 for each additional book: ____________________

TOTAL ENCLOSED ____________________

Name ____

Address____

City ____________________________State _____Zip __________

☐ Visa ☐ Mastercard ☐ American Express ☐ Discover

Credit card number ____

Expiration date ____

Ways to Order:

- Mailorder by credit card, personal check, or money order.
  Send to: Addicus Books, P.O. Box 45327, Omaha, NE 68145
- **Order TOLL FREE:** 800-352-2873
- **Visit us online at:** www.AddicusBooks.com
- **For discounts on bulk purchases, call our Special Sales Dept. at (402) 330-7493**